Stews
and
Ragouts

Stews
and
Ragouts

Simple and Hearty One-Dish Meals

by
Kay Shaw Nelson

Dover Publications, Inc., New York

Published in Canada by General Publishing Company, Ltd., 30 Lesmill Road, Don Mills, Toronto, Ontario.
Published in the United Kingdom by Constable and Company, Ltd., 10 Orange Street, London WC2H 7EG.

This Dover edition, first published in 1978, is a republication of the work first published in 1974 by Henry Regnery Co., under the title *Soups, Stews and Ragouts*. The section on soups has been omitted.

International Standard Book Number: 0-486-23662-5
Library of Congress Catalog Card Number: 79-51494

Manufactured in the United States of America
Dover Publications, Inc.
180 Varick Street
New York, N.Y. 10014

Contents

To my daughter,
Rae Katherine Nelson,
a convivial dining companion

CONVERSION TABLES FOR FOREIGN EQUIVALENTS

DRY INGREDIENTS

Ounces		Grams	Grams		Ounces	Pounds		Kilograms	Kilograms		Pounds
1	=	28.35	1	=	0.035	1	=	0.454	1	=	2.205
2		56.70	2		0.07	2		0.91	2		4.41
3		85.05	3		0.11	3		1.36	3		6.61
4		113.40	4		0.14	4		1.81	4		8.82
5		141.75	5		0.18	5		2.27	5		11.02
6		170.10	6		0.21	6		2.72	6		13.23
7		198.45	7		0.25	7		3.18	7		15.43
8		226.80	8		0.28	8		3.63	8		17.64
9		255.15	9		0.32	9		4.08	9		19.84
10		283.50	10		0.35	10		4.54	10		22.05
11		311.85	11		0.39	11		4.99	11		24.26
12		340.20	12		0.42	12		5.44	12		26.46
13		368.55	13		0.46	13		5.90	13		28.67
14		396.90	14		0.49	14		6.35	14		30.87
15		425.25	15		0.53	15		6.81	15		33.08
16		453.60	16		0.57						

LIQUID INGREDIENTS

Liquid Ounces		Milliliters	Milliliters		Liquid Ounces	Quarts		Liters	Liters		Quarts
1	=	29.573	1	=	0.034	1	=	0.946	1	=	1.057
2		59.15	2		0.07	2		1.89	2		2.11
3		88.72	3		0.10	3		2.84	3		3.17
4		118.30	4		0.14	4		3.79	4		4.23
5		147.87	5		0.17	5		4.73	5		5.28
6		177.44	6		0.20	6		5.68	6		6.34
7		207.02	7		0.24	7		6.62	7		7.40
8		236.59	8		0.27	8		7.57	8		8.45
9		266.16	9		0.30	9		8.52	9		9.51
10		295.73	10		0.33	10		9.47	10		10.57

Gallons (American)		Liters	Liters		Gallons (American)
1	=	3.785	1	=	0.264
2		7.57	2		0.53
3		11.36	3		0.79
4		15.14	4		1.06
5		18.93	5		1.32
6		22.71	6		1.59
7		26.50	7		1.85
8		30.28	8		2.11
9		34.07	9		2.38
10		37.86	10		2.74

INTRODUCTION

One snowy winter evening, while browsing through some books, I came across a marvelous salutation: "For soups and stews and choice ragouts Nell Cook was famous still."

Taken from the Ingoldsby Legends, a series of tales told by a parson under an assumed name and later discovered in the family chest, this tribute to Nell intrigued me. For even in 1842 when the Reverend Richard Barham had penned those lines, there must have been a proper appreciation for these delectable dishes.

Not knowing Nell's repertoire of recipes that had so impressed the parson, I set out to compile my own cosmopolitan collection of them. In particular I relished those one-pot or one-meal nourishing dishes of which even the plainest can be a creative combination, pleasing to both the eye and the palate. From my wanderings in various parts of the world I had not only acquired a great fondness for and appreciation of these dishes, but also a formidable number of recipes.

Of infinite variety and flavor, stews have no geographical boundaries. Each of the world's cuisines has some choice offerings. Many are robust and hearty familiar creations while others are refined unknown dishes with foreign names. On the other hand, we think of ragouts as belonging to the French, and like much of their cookery, consider them a little more special than other stews. They are perfect for special-occasion meals.

While stews and ragouts are age-old favorites they have particular appeal for the contemporary cook. Utensils, for example, are simple. All you need is a pot or kettle, some spoons and knives, and depending on how intricate the preparation, perhaps a few helpful gadgets. Most kitchens have all the necessary equipment.

Shopping for the ingredients poses no great problem as most items are readily available at the nearby supermarket. And in times when all of us are concerned about food prices, these one-dish meals can well be considered as boons to the budget. No worthy dish can be put together for a few cents, but in comparison to other choices, these selections can be prepared without investing considerable sums. Most of the fare is good and honest and is improved by seasoning and slow cooking. Even the more expensive ones will "go further" because of the type of cookery they are.

Preparation time can vary from several minutes to an hour or more, depending on the recipe. But, with few exceptions, all of the work, including the cooking, can be done ahead and the dish either kept in the refrigerator or frozen. Ragouts and stews reheat beautifully. For some there are "last minute" additions such as vegetables and egg yolks or other thickeners. Even so, these are no great effort.

Stews and ragouts will appeal to carefree cooks who want to welcome and mingle with guests, if entertaining, or have time with the family before the meal. None of the dishes suffers terribly if left on the stove a few minutes longer than planned.

With dishes like these you do not need much else on the menu. Some type of bread is usually a good accompaniment, along with a salad or vegetable. Appetizers or first courses are optional; desserts can be purchased or easily made. To aid in meal planning a menu suggestion is given with each recipe. Generally, this type of fare generates an air of conviviality and the meal is thus relaxed and pleasurable.

There is no magic or mystique about cooking stews and ragouts. All that you need is some time and effort for which you will be well rewarded. To assist in the preparation and cooking of these dishes, some helpful hints are offered in forthcoming pages. A glossary appears at the back of the book.

Throughout the book the recipes have been planned to provide fare that is not only appealing, but which is an interesting variation on the usual culinary repertoire. Some dishes are familiar; others are not. In serving them the cook may not acquire the fame of Nell Cook, but she will receive the warm appreciation of those who are bound to enjoy hearty stews and ritzy ragouts.

SOME HELPFUL HINTS

Although it is sometimes difficult to make distinctions between stews and ragouts, there are some basic differences in these substantial dishes.

Stews are made by covering the food with liquid and cooking in a tightly covered heavy pot or casserole at a low temperature, either in the oven or over direct heat. The cooking is generally lengthy as the purpose is to tenderize the foods and to make them more palatable by retaining the juices. Meat stews are either brown or white. For the former the meat is browned before cooking in liquid, while for the latter it is not. Stews are generally quite thick, containing rich sauces derived from the slow cooking or from the addition of thickening agents.

Ragouts are more complicated and fancier variations of stews, and are usually of French origin. Generally they are highly seasoned and often include wine.

Raw Materials

Necessary ingredients for stews and ragouts will, of, course, vary according to the recipe. One general rule applies to the selection of all of them. The finer the quality of foods and liquids, the better the dish. This does not necessarily mean the most expensive choices, but it is advisable to take time to select fresh food that is in prime condition. There are substitutes available for broths, stocks and bouillons, but those made from scratch will add much more flavor to the dish. If wine is used, it too should be of good quality.

The cuts of meat used for these dishes are often less tender and less expensive, such as beef shank, neck, shin, brisket, short ribs, flank and chuck; veal breast, shoulder, and shank; pork loin and shoulder; and lamb breast, neck, shoulder and riblets. These cuts will require longer cooking than poultry, seafood and vegetables.

Most of the essential ingredients can be easily found in supermarkets and neighborhood groceries, but for some recipes it may be necessary to obtain items at specialty food stores.

Cooking Equipment

Stews and ragouts can be made in a variety of pots, kettles, baking dishes or casseroles. The size will vary according to the recipe. Generally the cooking utensil should be heavy and large, with a tight-fitting cover. It should be determined whether the dish can be used for cooking over direct heat (or on top of the stove) as well as in the oven. Some utensils are suitable for both types of cookery; others are not.

A large kettle or French *marmite* can be used for making broths and stocks.

For stews and ragouts it is desirable to have a flame-proof, heavy-bottomed pan, kettle or casserole. Pans made of heavy copper or enamelled cast iron are best as they retain the heat during long, slow cooking and the food will not burn. Other good ones are made of stainless steel with a base of some metal such as copper. There are also utensils of earthenware, pottery, Pyrex, and other heat-proof materials that are oval, round or rectangular. Some of these, however, cannot withstand direct heat. Special dishes that can be purchased in some department stores or gourmet shops include the

French enamelled cast iron *cocottes* and earthenware or metal *daubières*.

Other necessary equipment includes knives and wooden boards for chopping, can or jar openers, measuring cups and spoons, a beater or whisk, a sieve or strainer, mixing bowls, skillets, one or more large cooking spoons, a slotted spoon or skimmer, a long-handled fork, a garlic press, a food mill and a larding needle.

Preparation and Cooking

For the best results, great care should be accorded the preparation and cooking of each dish. Some will take longer than others, but most of the work can be done beforehand. It is up to the cook whether she wishes to make her own stock or broth and cut up the meat. These preparations involve time and effort, but many persons prefer to do them. While it is not difficult to cup up most meats, cleaning and cutting fish and poultry is a little more messy and complicated. Thus, this can be done by the butcher or fish dealer. The preparation of vegetables and other ingredients does not generally present any great problems.

Some recipes call for marinating the meat in a seasoned liquid to tenderize it. Others suggest larding lean cuts by inserting strips of fat into the flesh with a larding needle. The latter will increase the juiciness of the meat. If the meat is to be browned, it should be wiped dry or it will steam instead. Add only a few pieces at a time and keep the pieces separate while browning. Do not pierce the meat with a fork while it is cooking or desirable juices will escape. After a preliminary browning, some stews are deglazed by flaming alcohol, such as brandy, before the addition of the liquid and other ingredients.

The most important step in stewing meat or other foods is to dissolve the food juices into the heated liquid in which they are cooked. Thus the first step in the cooking of a stew is very important. The liquid should be slowly brought to a simmer, just so that it bubbles occasionally, and then left to cook as slowly as possible. This is important because if the liquid boils the meat will become tough and not taste properly. All meat shrinks while cooking, but lower temperatures reduce the loss. The length of the cooking time will vary for the type and cut of meat, but the best way to be sure that it is properly done is to test it. It is not possible to give precise cooking times. Those in the recipes are to be used as guide lines.

Vegetables and other ingredients are added to ragouts and stews at various intervals during the cooking. Generally they require less time than meats and should not be overdone as they will lose their shape and color. To improve the flavor of some stews, vegetables or other seasonings are first sautéed in fat.

Once a stew has cooked, it is necessary to remove any fat that has collected on the surface. This may be done with a slotted spoon, skimmer or pieces of paper toweling while the liquid is still hot, or the dish may be cooled and refrigerated and the solidified fat lifted off.

For some stews it may be necessary to correct the final sauce by thinning it with more stock, wine or other liquid. It can be thickened by boiling down or adding *beurre manié* (tiny balls of flour and butter), cornstarch, arrowroot, or egg yolks and cream. If a stew is refrigerated or frozen, it is advisable to adjust the sauce after it has been reheated. These dishes are not difficult to reheat, but should be checked so that none of the ingredients becomes overdone and lose its proper form and color.

Flavorings

Most of the dishes in this international collection are flavorful well-seasoned creations that are designed to conform as closely as possible to the taste prevalent in their place of origin. Thus garlic and onions are liberally added to dishes from Mediterranean locales and sour cream and dill are featured in those of Eastern Europe. Ginger and soy sauce appear often in many of the Oriental recipes. The cook may wish, however, to alter some of these flavorings by using lesser amounts, such as one instead of two cloves of garlic or a smaller quantity of chili powder. This is her option. It is also helpful to know that various brands of some flavorings will vary in strength. This is especially true for curry powders and soy sauces. It is preferable to taste each dish to determine the desired flavor.

A wide variety of herbs and spices is used in stews and ragouts. These should be added with caution as a small amount may go a long way. If it is necessary to substitute dried herbs for fresh ones, remember that the latter are less pungent. As a guideline, use 1/2 teaspoon of a dried herb to replace each tablespoon of a fresh one.

Freezing

Many of the dishes in this collection can be satisfactorily frozen. In fact, in some cases the cook may wish to double or triple the ingredients so that what is not needed immediately can be put in the freezer.

If dishes are to be frozen, be careful not to overcook them as each will undergo additional cooking when reheated. It may be advisable to shorten the specified time by five or ten minutes.

In order to save space, stocks and broths can be boiled down to concentrates. Using the concentrate for flavoring, additional liquid can be added later. Cooked foods and liquids to be frozen should be cooled quickly and thoroughly and then put into appropriate containers, leaving an inch at the top to allow for expansion. Some baking dishes can be used for freezing and then transferred directly to the stove for reheating. Stews may be stored from two or four months, depending on the ingredients.

It is advisable to add some foods to these dishes after they have been defrosted and reheated. Among them are potatoes, dumplings, pasta and vegetables such as green peppers, green peas, lima beans and corn. Try to season a particular fare lightly so the seasonings can be checked and corrected after reheating. If a liquid is to be thickened with *beurre manie*, add this also after the dish is reheated and just before serving.

Frozen dishes may be thawed at room temperature or by placing the containers under running hot water. Reheat over low heat in a covered dish on the top of the stove or in a moderate (325°F.) oven. Frozen food can be slowly reheated without thawing but, of course, this takes longer.

Bouillons, Broths and Stocks

Many recipes for stews call for the use of bouillons, broths or stocks. These terms are often used interchangeably, since all three are produced by the same basic cooking process, boiling solid foods in seasoned liquids. The primary distinction is that bouillons and stocks are richer and more concentrated, the solid ingredients having been cooked to the point of discard, whereas broths are cooked for a shorter period and the solid foods are still usable.

In making stocks and bouillons, meat, poultry, fish or vegetables are slowly simmered in seasoned liquids. Bones are generally included in most of them as they provide necessary strength and gelatin. During the very slow cooking process all the nutrients and flavors are extracted from the solid foods. The selection of the ingredients, therefore, is very important and should include those which contain the necessary elements. The flesh of older animals contains more flavor than that of younger ones. Red meats yield more taste than white. Seasoning, particularly with salt, must be done carefully or the end product will acquire an undesirable flavor. After cooking, the remnants of the solid ingredients are discarded, and the remaining liquid must be properly degreased and, in some cases, clarified.

Broths are also acquired by simmering foods in seasoned liquids, but the process is not as lengthy nor is the aim to extract all the goodness from the ingredients, which are sometimes served in the broth.

Today it is not absolutely necessary to go through the time and effort of making one's own bouillon, stock or broth. Supermarkets carry ample supplies of beef bouillon and chicken broth, in either canned, powdered or tablet form, and canned or bottled clam juice is a good substitute for fish broth. These can easily be kept on hand. Concentrated bouillon liquid and cubes, however, are not recommended for long, slow cooking as they make the dish too salty. The homemade products are always superior in flavor and body, however, and can be made in large quantity and stored in the refrigerator or freezer to be used as needed.

Recipes for several of the basic liquids follow.

Brown Stock (or Bouillon)

2 pounds marrow bones, cracked
4 pounds shin or neck of beef, cut in small pieces
12 cups cold water
1/2 cup chopped celery
1/2 cup diced carrots
1/2 cup chopped onion
1 medium bay leaf
3 parsley sprigs
1/4 teaspoon dried thyme
1/4 teaspoon dried marjoram
6 whole cloves
8 peppercorns, bruised
1 tablespoon salt

Brown stock will have a richer color if the bones and/or meat are browned first. There are two methods of doing this. One is to put the cracked bones in a preheated hot oven (450°F.) for about 25 minutes, turning once or twice, or until well browned. They are then put in a large kettle with the other ingredients. The other is to scrape the marrow from the bones and put it in a large kettle. Then the marrow is heated and half of the pieces of meat browned in it. Add the bones, remaining meat and water. Put over moderate heat and bring slowly to a simmer. With a spoon or skimmer, take off all the foaming scum that has risen to the top. Add the remaining ingredients and bring very slowly to a simmer. Leave over very low heat, partially covered, for about 3 hours, or until all the possible goodness has been extracted from the ingredients. Stir occasionally while simmering. When the cooking is finished, strain the liquid and degrease it. This may be done by letting the stock settle for about 5 minutes and then removing the fat with a spoon, skimmer or paper towel. Or the stock can be cooled and put in the refrigerator until the fat hardens. Then it may be lifted or scraped off the top. The stock can be kept in the refrigerator or put in containers and frozen or may be frozen in freezer trays to produce cubes. If kept in the refrigerator for several days, it should be brought to a boil every day or so. Makes a little over 8 cups.

White Stock

Substitute cracked veal bones and veal knuckle or shank meat for the marrow bones and beef in the Brown Stock recipe.

Chicken Stock (or Bouillon or Broth)

1 stewing chicken, 4 to 5 pounds, cut up
12 cups cold water
1/3 cup each of diced carrots, celery and onions
1 leek, white part only, cleaned and sliced (optional)
2 sprigs parsley
1 small bay leaf
1/2 teaspoon dried thyme
2 teaspoons salt
6 whole peppercorns, bruised

Wash and wipe dry the chicken and put in a large kettle. Add the water and slowly bring to a simmer. With a spoon or skimmer remove any scum. Add the vegetables and seasonings and simmer very gently, covered, about 2½ hours. While simmering occasionally remove any scum. Strain. Remove the fat on the surface with a spoon or skimmer. Cool and put in the refrigerator until the fat hardens on the surface. Remove the fat and strain again. Store in the refrigerator up to 5 days or pour into containers and freeze. Makes a little over 8 cups.

Note: The chicken can be discarded or used for hash or other dishes.

Fish Stock

2 pounds white-fleshed fish with bones and trimmings
8 cups cold water
1 medium-sized onion, peeled and sliced thinly
1 medium-sized carrot, scraped and sliced thinly
2 whole cloves
1 bay leaf
1/2 teaspoon dried thyme
4 parsley sprigs
1 teaspoon salt
10 white or black peppercorns, bruised
1/2 lemon, sliced

Put all the ingredients in a kettle. Bring slowly to a simmer and skim. Cook very slowly, uncovered, for 1 hour. Strain and cool. Refrigerate or pour into containers to freeze. Makes about 6 cups. (1/2 or 1 cup of dry white wine and/or 1/3 cup of chopped mushroom stems can be added to the ingredients, if desired.)

STEWS

Since people first began devising mixtures of their favorite foods to be cooked in pots, there has been a close affinity between soups and stews. In fact they have been so closely allied that it is still difficult to make a distinction between them. Spain's *olla podrida* is called a soup and a stew. Suffice it to say that both dishes are made of cut-up ingredients cooked in liquid, but a stew is generally simmered longer and slower, and has less liquid.

Over the years, stews have ranked high in our diet, but unfortunately their reputation has sometimes suffered. Too often many persons merely think of a stew as uninspired mundane fare to be eaten as a last choice. Nothing could be further from the truth. Stews are actually gastronomic delights of fascinating variety that can be proudly served on any occasion.

The earliest stews were made with bits of meat or game with legumes and perhaps vegetables and seasonings. They provided necessary sustenance. Trying to improve them, the Romans combined bizarre mixtures so heavily spiced that the taste of the foods was disguised. Yet they did create the early versions of fricassees and ragouts.

To the French we are indebted for the refinements of stewing foods. By the twelfth century French chefs had succeeded in converting basic dishes to more sophisticated fare and bequeathed to the world the glorious *blanquettes, daubes, navarins, matelotes*, fricassees and ragouts—all stews.

One could travel around the world just sampling national stews, important to every cuisine. Cooks in other lands created such well-known kinds as goulashes, or the ubiquitous stew known variously as *stifado, estofado* or *estouffade*, to name only a few.

As stews, particularly those from foreign lands, have become more and more popular on the American table so have the array of utensils for cooking them. Although any heavy pot of the right size is adequate, many persons delight in using fancier kinds of varying shapes and colors. Some of the most attractive are imported and have such esoteric-sounding names as *daubière* or *braisière*. Most are so appealing that the stew can be served as well as cooked in the pot.

It's great fun to entertain with stews—they generate an informal or casual mood, and the serving can be most flexible, either with informal or formal appointments. Often the hostess can create a particular atmosphere with the table decor to fit in with the theme of a foreign menu or a particular occasion. Stews are perfect for buffets, dinners or suppers, as well as noon-time meals. The following recipes with menu suggestions will be rewarding to cook and serve.

Blanquette de Veau

Of French origin, this well-known, lemon-flavored veal stew with small white onions and fresh mushrooms is superb fare. It takes some time and effort to prepare, and except for the final addition of egg yolks and cream, it can be made ahead and reheated just before the meal. It is excellent for a company dinner.

2½ pounds boneless veal shoulder, cut into 2-inch cubes
4 cups beef bouillon or water
1 carrot, scraped and chopped
1 medium-sized onion stuck with 2 whole cloves
1 leek, white part only, cleaned and sliced (optional)
bouquet garni (1 bay leaf, 1/2 teaspoon dried thyme,
2 parsley sprigs)
salt, pepper to taste
5 tablespoons butter
16 small white onions, peeled
1/2 cup water
18 fresh mushrooms
2 tablespoons fresh lemon juice   ·
3 tablespoons flour
2 egg yolks
1/2 cup heavy cream
freshly grated nutmeg to taste

Put the veal and bouillon in a large kettle. Bring to a boil and skim. Add the carrot, onion with cloves, leek, *bouquet garni*, salt and pepper. Lower the heat and cook slowly, covered, for 1½ hours, skimming from time to time. While the veal is cooking, melt 1 tablespoon butter in a saucepan. Add the white onions and sauté 1 minute. Pour in the water and cook the onions, covered, until just tender, about 10 minutes. Drain and set aside. Clean the mushrooms and cut into halves lengthwise. Sauté in 2 tablespoons butter and 1 tablespoon lemon juice for 5 minutes. Remove from the heat and set aside. When the veal has finished cooking, re- move from the stove. Take out the meat. Strain 2 cups of the liquid and set aside. (Discard any remaining liquid and the vegetables in which the veal was cooked.) Melt 2 table- spoons butter in a large saucepan. Add the flour and cook, stirring, one minute. Gradually add the strained meat liquid and cook, stirring, until the sauce is thickened and smooth. Combine the egg yolks and cream and beat lightly. Mix a small amount of the hot sauce with the egg yolks. Return the mix- ture to the sauce. Cook slowly, stirring often, until thickened. Season with salt, pepper and nutmeg. Add the reserved veal, onions, mushrooms and drippings and the remaining 1 tablespoon of lemon juice. Leave on the stove long enough to heat through. Serves 6.

MENU

Blanquette de Veau
Buttered Noodles
Mixed Green Salad
French Pastry

Hungarian Pork Tokany

In the superb repertoire of Hungarian stews, one of the best is called *tokany*. A paprika-flavored pork or beef dish for which the meat is cut into strips, a *tokany* also includes mushrooms, vegetables and sour cream.

**2 pounds lean boneless pork, cut into
3-by-1-inch strips
1/4 cup lard or shortening
salt, pepper to taste
1 tablespoon paprika
1 large onion, peeled and chopped
1 large carrot, scraped and sliced thinly
1 large green pepper, cleaned and sliced
2 medium-sized tomatoes, peeled and chopped
2 cups sliced fresh mushrooms
1 tablespoon flour
1 cup sour cream, at room temperature**

Wipe the pork dry and brown it in the lard in a large saucepan. Season with salt and pepper. Add the paprika and onion and cook 1 minute. Cover and cook slowly for 30 minutes. Add the carrot, pepper and tomatoes and cook another 30 minutes or until tender. Stir in the mushrooms 10 minutes before the cooking is finished. Add the flour and sour cream and cook over low heat, stirring, until thickened and smooth, about 5 minutes. Serves 6.

MENU

Hungarian Pork Tokany
Buttered Noodles
Wilted Cucumber Salad
Warm Poppy-Seed Rolls
Fruit-Filled Pancakes

Turkish Gardeners' Stew

The Turks prepare a marvelous stew called *turlu*, which is made from lamb and a medley of vegetables. The choice of vegetables will vary as to what is in season and available, but the ones in this recipe are a typical selection. It is a good summer dinner dish.

4 medium-sized onions, peeled and sliced
1/2 cup butter or margarine
2 pounds boneless shoulder or leg of lamb, cut into
1-inch cubes
salt, pepper to taste
4 medium-sized zucchini, washed and sliced
2 medium-sized eggplant, stemmed and cubed
1 pound fresh green beans, stemmed and cut up
1/2 pound fresh okra, stemmed and cut up
4 large tomatoes, peeled and chopped

Sauté the onions in the butter in a large kettle until tender. Wipe the lamb dry and brown on all sides. Season with salt and pepper. Cover with about 1/2 cup water and cook slowly for about 1 hour. Add more water while cooking if necessary to prevent sticking. Add the prepared vegetables and continue to cook slowly, covered, about 30 minutes longer or until the ingredients are cooked. Serves 6.

MENU

Turkish Gardeners' Stew
Hot Boiled Rice
Crusty Dark Bread
Chilled Watermelon

Philippine Adobo

The Filipinos have a rich heritage of national stews which are served traditionally at festive meals. This highly seasoned chicken and pork *adobo* is better if prepared two or three days in advance and reheated.

**1 frying chicken, about 2½ pounds, cut up
2 pounds boneless pork loin or shoulder, cut into
1-inch cubes
1 cup wine vinegar
1/2 cup soy sauce
2 bay leaves
2-3 garlic cloves
1 teaspoon peppercorns, slightly bruised
salt to taste
lard or oil for frying
1 cup coconut milk***

Put the chicken pieces, pork, vinegar, soy sauce, bay leaves, garlic, peppercorns and salt in a large kettle, cover and leave to marinate at room temperature for 1½ to 2 hours. Put the mixture on the stove and bring to a boil. Lower the heat, cover and cook very slowly for about 45 minutes or until the meat is tender. Remove the pork and chicken and drain. Strain the liquid and reserve. Fry the pork cubes and chicken in the lard or oil to brown on all sides. Return the liquid to the kettle. Add the coconut milk and cook slowly about 10 minutes longer, or until the mixture thickens. Serves 8.
*See recipe on page 34.

MENU

Philippine Adobo
Hot Cooked Rice
Warm Corn Sticks
Pineapple Cream Pie

Corsican Pebronata de Boeuf

Despite French and Italian influences, the cuisine of the Mediterranean island of Corsica is individualistic. Among its traditional dishes are a number of hearty well seasoned stews. One of the best, *pebronata*, is made in large quantity and can be prepared beforehand and reheated. This is a good buffet dish.

2 large onions, peeled and chopped
3-4 medium-sized garlic cloves, crushed
2/3 cup olive or vegetable oil
2 bay leaves, crumbled
1 teaspoon dried thyme
salt, pepper to taste
5 pounds boneless lean beef (rump, chuck, top or bottom
round), cut into 1½-inch cubes
1/4 cup flour
2 cups (about) dry red wine
2 teaspoons (about) ground red peppers or hot sauce
1 cup tomato sauce
1 teaspoon dried oregano

Sauté the onions and garlic in the oil in a large kettle until the onions are tender. Add the bay leaves, thyme, salt and pepper; cook 1 minute. Push aside and add the beef cubes, wiped dry, several at a time, to brown on all sides. Sprinkle with the flour and mix well. Add the wine, cover and cook slowly for 1 hour. Add the red peppers, varying the amount according to taste, tomato sauce, oregano and more wine, if needed. Continue to cook slowly for another 30 minutes, or until the meat is tender. The final sauce should be quite thick. Serves 12.

MENU

Corsican Pebronata de Boeuf
Hot Cooked Macaroni
French Bread
Escarole Salad
Peaches in White Wine

Osso Buco Milanese

This well-known specialty from Milan, Italy, means "hollow bones." One of the delights in eating the bones or shanks is to extract the marrow with a spoon. A combination of chopped garlic, parsley and grated lemon peel called *gremolata*, is important to this dish. It is a good dish for a company sit-down dinner.

**8 meaty veal shanks or shins with marrow in the bones,
cut into 2½-inch pieces
flour
salt, pepper to taste
1/3 cup (about) butter, olive or vegetable oil
1 cup chopped onion
2 large garlic cloves, crushed
1 cup dry white wine
1½ cups canned Italian plum tomatoes,
drained and chopped
1/2 cup (about) beef broth or bouillon
bouquet garni (1 bay leaf, 1/2 teaspoon dried thyme,
2 parsley sprigs)
1 tablespoon grated lemon peel
3 tablespoons chopped fresh parsley**

Wipe the veal shanks or shins dry and dust with the flour seasoned with salt and pepper. Heat the butter or oil in a heavy kettle or casserole and brown the meat pieces, a few at a time, on all sides. As they are cooked, transfer to a platter. Sauté the onion and 1 garlic clove in the drippings until tender, adding more butter if needed. Arrange the shanks to stand upright over the onions. Add the wine, tomatoes, broth or bouillon, and *bouquet garni*. Bring to a boil. Reduce the heat, cover and cook slowly for 1½ to 2 hours, until the meat is tender. Add a little more broth during the cooking, if needed. When the cooking is finished, combine the remaining garlic clove, the lemon peel and parsley, and sprinkle over the ingredients. Correct the seasoning and remove and discard the bay leaf and parsley. Serves 6.

MENU

Osso Buco Milanese
Risotto Milanese or Buttered Rice
Hearts of Lettuce Salad
Bread Sticks
Lemon Sherbet with Chocolate Shavings

Swiss Berner Platte

This national Swiss favorite, named for the charming capital of Berne, is a fascinating, large platter of sauerkraut and a wide variety of meats with vegetable accompaniments. It is fun to serve for an informal sit-down dinner or late supper.

2 pounds sauerkraut
2 tablespoons bacon or pork fat
2 medium-sized onions, peeled and chopped
8 peppercorns
10 juniper berries
salt to taste
2½ cups dry white wine
1/2 pound bacon in one piece
6 smoked pork chops

1 pound pork sausage links, cooked and drained
6 bratwurst or knockwurst, braised and drained
6 thick slices cooked ham
3 cups cooked and drained hot green beans
3 tablespoons butter or margarine
1 garlic clove, minced
pepper to taste
6 medium-sized potatoes, boiled, drained and peeled

Rinse the sauerkraut and drain well to remove all the liquid. Heat the fat in a large kettle. Add the onions and sauté until tender. Add the sauerkraut and sauté about 5 minutes, mixing with a fork. Add the peppercorns, juniper berries, salt, wine and bacon. Cover and cook slowly for 1 hour. Add the pork chops, sausage, bratwurst and ham and continue cooking for another 30 minutes longer, or until all the ingredients are cooked. Remove and discard the peppercorns and juniper berries. Combine the hot green beans, butter and garlic and season with salt and pepper. To serve, spoon the sauerkraut onto a large platter and surround with the meats. Put the potatoes in a bowl and the green beans in another dish; serve with the *platte*. Serves 6.

MENU

Swiss Berner Platte
Hard Rolls
Apple Tarts or Pie

Carbonnade à la Flamande

A beef and onion stew flavored with beer, brown sugar and herbs is traditional fare in Belgium's northern region of Flanders. The name is believed to have derived from the French word for carbon which means broiled or grilled over coals or charcoal.

3 pounds lean boneless beef chuck or round steak, cut
into 2-inch strips
flour
salt, pepper to taste
1/2 cup lard or butter
4 large onions, peeled and thinly sliced
1-2 garlic cloves, crushed
bouquet garni (1 bay leaf, 1/2 teaspoon crumbled dried
thyme, 4 sprigs fresh parsley, all wrapped in cheesecloth)
2 tablespoons brown sugar
2½ cups (about) light beer
2 tablespoons red wine vinegar
12 boiled medium-sized potatoes
3 tablespoons chopped fresh parsley

Wipe the meat dry and dredge each strip with flour seasoned with salt and pepper. Set aside. Heat the lard or butter
in a kettle and sauté the onions and garlic in it until tender.
Push aside and add the meat, several strips at a time. Brown
on all sides. Tie the bay leaf, thyme and parsley in a small
square of cheesecloth to make a *bouquet garni*. Add to the
ingredients. Mix in the sugar and beer. Season with salt and
pepper. Cover and cook over low heat about 1½ hours or
until the meat is tender. Add more beer while cooking, if
needed. (The liquid should cover the ingredients while cooking.) Remove and discard the *bouquet garni*. Stir in the vinegar
just before serving. Serve the hot boiled potatoes, garnished
with the parsley, with the stew. Serves 8.

MENU

Carbonnade à la Flamande
Endive Salad
Warm Dinner Rolls
Apricot Tart

Pacific Seafood Stew

This American stew includes a number of seafood treasures that are taken from the Pacific Ocean. It is a good luncheon or supper dish.

1/3 cup vegetable oil
1 large onion, peeled and chopped
1-2 medium-sized garlic cloves, crushed
2 tablespoons tomato paste
2 cups fish broth, bottled clam broth or water
2 cups (about) dry white wine
1 medium-sized bay leaf
1/2 teaspoon dried basil or thyme
3 parsley sprigs
salt, pepper to taste
1 quart hard-shell clams, washed and scrubbed well
1 pound halibut, cut into 2-inch pieces*
1 pound salmon, cut into 2-inch pieces
1 pound lump crabmeat, cleaned
1/4 cup chopped fresh parsley

Heat the oil in a large kettle and sauté the onions and garlic in it until tender. Stir in the tomato paste. Add the broth, wine, bay leaf, basil or thyme, parsley sprigs, salt or pepper and bring to a boil. Lower the heat and cook slowly, covered, for 30 minutes. Add the clams, halibut, salmon and crabmeat and more wine, if desired. Cover and continue to cook slowly about 12 minutes or until the clams have opened and the fish is tender. Remove and discard the bay leaf and parsley sprigs. Add the chopped parsley. Serves 6.
*An equivalent amount of any other kind of white-fleshed fish can be substituted for the halibut, if desired.

MENU

Pacific Seafood Stew
Warm Sourdough Bread

Romaine Lettuce Salad
Blackberry Pie

Coq au Vin

This popular dish, whose French name means simply *chicken in wine*, is made in several variations, but generally includes small white onions and mushrooms. It is a good dish for a Saturday night dinner.

2 frying chickens, about 2½ pounds each, cut up
salt, pepper to taste
10 tablespoons butter or margarine
4 tablespoons (about) olive oil
1 medium-sized piece lean bacon, diced
3 pounds small white onions, peeled
1½ pounds fresh mushrooms, cleaned
1/2 cup brandy
4 cups dry red wine
1/2 teaspoon dried thyme
2 bay leaves
4 parsley sprigs
4 medium-sized garlic cloves, crushed
1/4 cup flour
1/3 cup chopped fresh parsley

Wash the chicken and pat dry. Season with salt and pepper. Set aside. Heat 6 tablespoons of the butter, the oil and the bacon in a large kettle or casserole. Add the onions and sauté about 10 minutes or less, depending on their size. Remove the onions with a slotted spoon and set aside. Add the mushrooms to the drippings and sauté 5 minutes, adding more oil if needed. Remove and set aside. Add the chicken pieces to the drippings and fry until golden on all sides. Pour in the brandy and ignite it. Let burn, shaking the pan, until the flames subside. Return the onions to the kettle. Add the wine, thyme, bay leaves, parsley and garlic. Season with salt and pepper. Bring to a boil. Lower the heat, cover and cook slowly, about

30 minutes or until the chicken is tender. Add the mushrooms during the last 5 minutes of cooking. Blend together 4 tablespoons of softened butter and the flour. Shape into tiny balls and add to the liquid. Stir with a whisk or spoon until well blended. Arrange the chicken, onions and mushrooms on a platter. Cover with the sauce. Garnish with the parsley. Serves 8.

MENU

Coq au Vin
Parsley Potatoes
Hearts of Lettuce Salad
French Bread
Fresh Strawberries and Cream

Hungarian Szekely Goulash

Over the years several variations of Hungary's national stew, *gulyás*, have emerged. One of the best includes sauerkraut and is sometimes called Transylvanian goulash, having been named for a region which is now a part of Rumania. It is a good winter dinner or supper dish.

**3 pounds boneless lean pork (or a mixture of 1 pound
boneless beef chuck, 1 pound boneless veal and
1 pound boneless lean pork), cut into 1½-inch cubes
2 tablespoons (about) lard or other fat
2 large onions, peeled and sliced thinly
2 tablespoons paprika
1½ teaspoons caraway seeds
salt, pepper to taste
3 pounds sauerkraut, drained and rinsed
2 cups sour cream at room temperature
1 pound thin egg noodles, cooked and drained (optional)
3 tablespoons butter or margarine (optional)**

Cut any fat from the meat and discard it. Brown the meat

in the lard in a large kettle, adding about 1 pound at a time. Remove to a plate after it is browned. Add the onion slices to the kettle, as well as more lard, if needed, and sauté until tender. Stir in the paprika and cook 1 minute. Return the meat to the kettle. Add the caraway seeds, salt, pepper and enough water to cover the ingredients. Cook slowly, covered, for 1 hour. Add the sauerkraut and more water, if needed, and continue to cook slowly about 30 minutes longer or until the meat is tender. Mix in the sour cream and leave on the stove just long enough to heat through. Serve with the noodles, mixed with the butter, if desired. Serves 8.

MENU

Hungarian Szekely Goulash
Hot Buttered Noodles
Rye Bread
Sliced Cucumber Salad
Nut Cake

Carbonada Criolla

South Americans are fond of this flavorful meat and fruit stew, which is sometimes baked and served in a large pumpkin instead of a kettle. It is a good winter dinner dish.

1/4 cup vegetable oil
1 large onion, peeled and chopped
1 garlic clove, crushed
2 pounds stew beef, cut into 1½-inch cubes
1 can (1 pound) tomatoes
1 bay leaf
1/2 teaspoon dried oregano
salt, pepper to taste
1 cup beef broth or bouillon
1 pound sweet potatoes, peeled and cubed
2 cups cubed butternut or acorn squash
1 large green pepper, cleaned and cut into strips

1 cup fresh or frozen corn niblets
1 cup diced fresh or canned peaches
1 medium-sized tart apple, pared, cored and diced

Heat the oil in a large kettle. Add the onions and garlic and sauté until tender. Push aside and add the beef cubes, several at a time, and brown on all sides. Remove to a plate if necessary. Add the tomatoes, bay leaf, oregano, salt and pepper; cook 1 minute. Pour in the broth and bring to a boil. Lower the heat and cook slowly, covered, for 1 hour. Add the sweet potatoes and squash and continue the cooking another 25 minutes or until the vegetables are just tender. Add the green pepper, corn, peaches and apple. Cook 5 minutes longer, or until the ingredients are tender. Serves 6.

MENU

Carbonada Criolla
Warm Cornbread
Strawberry Chiffon Pie

Viennese Chicken Paprikás

A superb chicken stew that probably had its origins in the kitchens of Hungary, chicken paprikás has long been popular fare in Vienna also. It is a good weekend luncheon dish.

2 frying chickens, about 2½ pounds each, cut up
salt, pepper to taste
1/3 cup (about) butter or margarine
2 large onions, peeled and sliced thinly
1-2 tablespoons paprika
2 large tomatoes, peeled and chopped
1 cup (about) chicken broth
2 tablespoons flour
2 cups heavy sweet cream or sour cream
at room temperature

Wash and pat dry the chicken pieces. Season with salt and pepper. Heat the butter in a kettle and brown the chicken, a few pieces at a time, on both sides over moderate heat. Remove from the kettle with tongs and keep warm. Add the sliced onions to the drippings and more butter, if needed. Sauté until tender. Stir in the paprika and cook 1 minute. Add the tomatoes and sauté until mushy, 1 or 2 minutes. Return the chicken pieces to the kettle. Add the broth. Cover and cook slowly for about 30 minutes or until the chicken is just tender. Add more broth while cooking, if needed. Remove the chicken pieces with tongs and keep warm. Scrape the drippings and stir in the flour. Gradually add the cream and cook, stirring, until thickened and smooth. Correct the seasoning. Add the chicken pieces, and leave on the stove long enough to warm through. Garnish the top with chopped fresh dill, if desired. Serves 6 to 8.

MENU

Viennese Chicken Paprikás
Buttered Noodles
Caraway-Flavored Cabbage Salad
Warm Poppy-Seed Rolls
Mocha Torte

Spanish Cocido

This hearty Spanish national stew is made in several regional variations. Always included in it are chickpeas (garbanzos), nutty flavored legumes, and a variety of vegetables and meats. This is a southern version that includes such typical foods as rice, tomatoes and green beans. The stew can be served in three courses: first, the broth, then, the vegetables, and lastly, the meats. This is a good buffet dish.

2 large onions, peeled and chopped
1/3 cup olive or vegetable oil
2 pounds stewing beef (rump, chuck, bottom or top round),

cut into 2-inch cubes
4 pounds beef soup bones with marrow
1/2 pound bacon in one piece
16 cups water
salt, pepper to taste
2 large carrots, scraped and diced
2 cans (1 pound, 4 ounces each) chickpeas, drained
6 large tomatoes, peeled and chopped
1½ cups uncooked rice
2 pounds Spanish sausages (chorizo) or
garlic sausages, sliced thinly
red pepper to taste
4 cups frozen green beans
pinch of saffron (optional)

Sauté the onions in the olive oil in a large kettle until tender. Push aside and add the beef cubes, a few at a time, and brown on all sides. Add the beef bones, bacon, water, salt and pepper. Bring to a boil. Lower the heat and cook slowly, covered, for 1 hour. Remove the cover and skim off any fat that has accumulated on the top. Add the carrots and cook 15 minutes. Stir in the chickpeas, tomatoes, rice, sausages and red pepper. Continue to cook about 20 minutes longer or until the ingredients are tender. Add the frozen beans 10 minutes before the cooking is finished. Stir in the saffron before removing from the heat. Remove the bones and take out any marrow left in them. Return the marrow to the stew and discard the bones. Serves 12.

MENU

Spanish Cocido
Warm Cornbread
Baked Custard

Balkan Veal-Barley Stew

Two very nourishing and appealing foods, barley and veal, are combined with seasonings and green beans to make this stew. It is a good Sunday supper dish.

4 pounds veal breast, cut into 2-inch pieces
4 tablespoons vegetable oil
1 large onion, peeled and chopped
2 medium-sized garlic cloves, crushed
salt, pepper to taste
1/2 teaspoon sugar
2 tablespoons all-purpose flour
4 cups beef bouillon
1 can (6 ounces) tomato paste
***bouquet garni* (1 bay leaf, 1/2 teaspoon dried thyme,**
2 parsley sprigs)
1 cup pearl barley
3 cups frozen cut-up green beans
1 tablespoon chopped fresh dill

Wipe the veal pieces dry. Heat 2 tablespoons of the oil in a large kettle. Add about half the veal and brown on all sides. Remove to a plate. Add the remaining 2 tablespoons of oil and the veal and brown. Remove also to the plate. Add the onion and garlic to the drippings in the kettle and sauté until tender. Return the veal pieces to the kettle. Season with salt and pepper. Add the sugar and sprinkle with the flour. Stir about so the flour is evenly distributed. Combine the bouillon and tomato paste and pour into the kettle. Add the *bouquet garni*. Bring to a boil. Lower the heat, cover and cook very slowly for 1 hour. Add the barley and continue cooking until it is tender, 45 minutes to 1 hour. Add the green beans 15 minutes before the cooking is finished. Stir in the dill. Remove and discard the bay leaf and parsley. Serves 8.

MENU

Balkan Veal-Barley Stew
Crusty Dark Bread
Yogurt-Cucumber Salad
Cooked Pear Compote

Rabbit Stew Provençale

Europeans, particularly the French, are fond of rich stews featuring hare or rabbit. One of the best is native to Provence and features such favorite foods as tomatoes, mushrooms, olives and herbs.

1 fresh or frozen rabbit, about 3 pounds, cut up
1/3 cup olive or vegetable oil
2 tablespoons butter or margarine
20 small white onions, peeled
2 garlic cloves, crushed
3 medium-sized tomatoes, peeled and chopped
1 bay leaf
1/2 teaspoon dried thyme
1/4 cup brandy (optional)
dry red or white wine
salt, pepper to taste
20 medium-sized fresh mushrooms, cleaned
20 pitted black olives
3 tablespoons chopped fresh parsley

Wash the rabbit pieces and wipe dry. Sauté in the oil and butter in a large kettle until golden on all sides. With tongs remove to a plate. To the drippings add the onions and sauté until tender. Add the garlic, tomatoes, bay leaf, thyme and brandy. Cook 2 minutes. Return the rabbit pieces to the kettle. Cover with wine and season with salt and pepper. Cook slowly, covered, about 30 minutes, or until the rabbit is tender. Add the mushrooms and olives after the dish has been cooking 20 minutes. Stir in the parsley just before serving. Serves 4.

MENU

Rabbit Stew Provençale
Parsley Boiled Potatoes

Beet Salad
Crusty French Bread
Cheese Plate

Polish Bigos

A very old and traditional Polish dish is *bigos* or hunters' stew. Originally it was made with vegetables such as cabbage, onions and mushrooms, apples and prunes, and an abundance of leftover cooked meats and game. Made in great quantity, *bigos* was featured at national holiday meals and parties following the customary hunts. Today this stew is made in many variations, generally with whatever ingredients are on hand. This version is a good buffet dish.

2 ounces dried brown mushrooms
1/4 pound salt pork or bacon, chopped
3 large onions, peeled and sliced thinly
1/2 pound (about 2½ cups) shredded cabbage
**1 pound lean beef (chuck, rump, bottom or top round),
cut into 1½-inch cubes**
1 pound lean pork, cut into 1½-inch cubes
3 pounds sauerkraut, washed and drained
3 medium-sized tart apples, peeled, cored and chopped
1 can (14½ ounces) whole tomatoes, undrained
1 cup vegetable broth or water
2 teaspoons sugar
2 teaspoons prepared sharp mustard
salt, pepper to taste
**1 pound smoked Polish sausage or *kielbasa*, cut into
1-inch rounds**
1/2 cup Madeira wine
12 medium-sized potatoes, washed and peeled
1/4 cup chopped fresh parsley

Soak the mushrooms in lukewarm water in a small bowl for 20 minutes. Drain, reserving the mushroom liquid. Press the mushrooms to release all the liquid. Chop and set aside. Put the chopped pork or bacon and sliced onions in a large kettle and sauté until tender. Add the cabbage and sauté about 3 minutes. Push aside and add the beef and pork cubes; brown on all sides. Mix the ingredients together in the kettle. Add the sauerkraut, apples, tomatoes, chopped mushrooms, reserved mushroom liquid, vegetable broth, sugar, mustard, salt and pepper. Cover and cook slowly for about 2 hours. Add the sausage during the last 1/2 hour of cooking. Stir in the Madeira just before removing from the heat. During the last stages of the cooking, boil the potatoes until just tender, and add to the stew or serve separately, sprinkled with the parsley. Serves 12.

Note: Substitute 1 cup sliced fresh or canned mushrooms for the dried ones, if desired.

MENU

Polish Bigos
Pumpernickel
Honey Cake

Chili Con Carne

Controversies rage over the proper ingredients and preparation of this well-known dish. Some enthusiasts include beans with the beef, tomatoes and chili peppers. Others do not. Seasonings vary considerably. There are those who advocate using only chili powder, and those who favor the addition of cayenne, oregano, cumin or garlic. This recipe is my favorite version. It can be made as spicy as the cook desires. It is a good weekday supper dish.

1 pound pinto beans
salt to taste
2 cups chopped onions
2 medium-sized garlic cloves, crushed
3 tablespoons (about) vegetable oil
2 pounds lean round or chuck beef, cut into 1½-inch cubes

1 can (1 pound, 12 ounces each) tomatoes, undrained
1-2 tablespoons chili powder
1/2 teaspoon ground cumin
1 teaspoon ground oregano
1/2 teaspoon crushed red peppers or cayenne
black pepper to taste

Put the beans in a large kettle or pot and cover with water. Leave to soak overnight or for about 9 hours. Bring the beans to a boil. Season with salt. Lower the heat and cook slowly, covered, until the beans are just tender, about 1¼ hours. Do not overcook. Add more water while cooking, if needed. Drain and set aside. Sauté the onions and garlic in the oil in a large kettle until tender. Push aside and add the meat cubes, about 1/2 pound at a time, and brown on all sides. Add more oil, if needed. Stir in the tomatoes and break them up with a spoon. Cook a few minutes, stirring, until the foods are well mixed. Add the remaining ingredients, cover and cook slowly for about 2 hours or until the meat is tender. Add the drained beans during the last 15 minutes of cooking. Serves 8.

MENU

Chili Con Carne
Hot Buttered Rice
Mixed Green Salad
Warm Tortillas
Orange Ambrosia

Curried Chicken From Thailand

Some of the best dishes to be found in the cuisines of Southeast Asian countries are those flavored with curry, a combination of several spices prepared in powder or paste form. The curries of Thailand, which are generally very hot and pungent, are so varied that they even have an intriguing range of colors made by blending various spices, herbs, condiments or other flavorings. The curry used for chicken is deep yellow and is made by combining turmeric, carda-mom, coriander, nutmeg and chilies, among other spices, with a strong fish sauce. Unfortunately it is not easy to dupli-cate these curries in an American home as the necessary native ingredients and implements are not available. This curry is an adaptation of the Thai version.

3 cups coconut milk
2 tablespoons curry paste
1 cup minced green onions, with tops
2 garlic cloves, crushed
1/3 cup peanut or vegetable oil
2 frying chickens, about 2½ pounds, cut up
1 teaspoon fresh lemon juice
8 cups hot boiled rice
condiments: grated coconut, crumbled cooked bacon,
sliced bananas, chutney, chopped green onions,
peanuts, pickles and green pepper

Prepare the coconut milk and curry paste with the recipes that follow. To make the curry, sauté the onions and garlic in the oil in a frying pan or kettle. Add 2 tablespoons of the curry paste and cook 1 minute. Add the chicken pieces, and more oil if necessary, and sauté on all sides until golden. Add the lemon juice and coconut milk and bring to a boil. Lower the heat, cover and cook slowly for about 35 minutes, or until the chicken is tender and the sauce is thickened. Serve with the rice and condiments, each in a separate small bowl. Serves 8.
Note: An easier but less flavorful version of this dish can be made by substituting curry powder for the curry paste.

Coconut Milk

Put 3 cups freshly grated or packaged or frozen unsweet-ened coconut and 3 cups of hot water in a bowl and leave for 10 minutes. Strain the liquid from the coconut, discarding the coconut. Use the "milk" as directed in the recipe.

Curry Paste

Combine 1 tablespoon ground coriander, 1 tablespoon turmeric, 1 teaspoon ground cumin, 1/2 teaspoon ground cardamom, 1/2 teaspoon chili powder and 1/2 teaspoon black pepper in a mortar or bowl and mix with a pestle or spoon to thoroughly combine. Add 2 tablespoons vinegar and 2 table-spoons anchovy paste and mix well. Makes 1/4 cup. (Save the leftover paste for another recipe.)

MENU

Curried Chicken From Thailand
Tossed Green Salad
Pineapple Sherbet with Crushed Pineapple

Israeli Beef Cholent

This traditional Jewish meal-in-one-dish of Central Euro-pean origin has long been prepared for the Sabbath meals when cooking is forbidden. The name is believed to have derived from the French word *chaud*, warm. It is an excellent supper dish.

1/2 pound dried lima beans
2 medium-sized onions, peeled and sliced
2 large carrots, scraped and sliced
3 tablespoons chicken fat or shortening
1/2 cup pearl barley
8 medium-sized potatoes, pared
2½-3 pounds brisket of beef
3 tablespoons brown sugar
salt, pepper to taste

Soak the beans in water to cover overnight or for about 9 hours. Sauté the onions and carrots in the fat in a large kettle for 5 minutes. Drain the beans and add them, the barley and potatoes. Push the ingredients aside and place the beef in the center. Cover with water and add the sugar, salt and pepper. Cover tightly and cook very slowly on top of the stove for about 2½ hours, or until the meat is tender. During the cooking shake the kettle occasionally to prevent the ingredients from sticking. Serves 8.

MENU

Israeli Beef Cholent
Sliced Tomato Salad
Dark Bread
Stewed Apricots with Cream

Navarin Printanier

Lamb stew prepared with a variety of spring vegetables is as attractive as it is delectable. In France it is made with fresh, tender and young vegetables, but it can also be prepared with frozen ones. Although generally baked in the oven, this dish also can be cooked on top of the stove. It is an excellent dish for a company dinner.

3 pounds lean lamb shoulder, cut into 2-inch cubes
3 tablespoons (about) butter or vegetable oil
1 tablespoon sugar
salt, pepper to taste
2 tablespoons flour
2 cups lamb or beef stock or bouillon
4 medium-sized tomatoes, peeled, seeded and chopped
2 garlic cloves, crushed
1 large bay leaf
1/4 teaspoon dried thyme
6 medium-sized carrots, scraped and cut into
1½-inch lengths
6 small turnips, peeled and cubed
12 small new potatoes or 6 medium-sized ones,

**peeled and cut up
16 small white onions, peeled
1 cup shelled fresh or frozen green peas
1 cup cut-up fresh or frozen green beans**

Wipe the lamb pieces dry and brown on all sides in the heated butter or oil in a large kettle. Add the sugar and leave over moderately high heat until it caramelizes, about 5 minutes. Season with salt and pepper and sprinkle the flour over the meat. Mix well. Pour in the stock or bouillon and add the tomatoes, garlic, bay leaf and thyme. Mix and bring to a boil. Lower the heat, cover and cook slowly for 1 hour. Take off the stove and spoon the meat onto a plate. Strain the sauce into a bowl. Wash the kettle in which the meat was cooked, and return the strained sauce to it. Add the carrots, turnips, potatoes and onions. Cover and cook slowly until the vegetables are just tender, about 25 minutes. Add the peas and green beans and cook about another 10 minutes, or until tender. (If frozen vegetables are used, add them during the last 5 minutes of cooking.) To serve, arrange the ingredients on a large platter. Serves 8.

MENU

*Navarin Printanier
Romaine Salad
Crusty French Bread
Orange or Pineapple Bavarian Cream*

Portuguese Seafood Stew

In the villages along the Portuguese Atlantic coast, a favorite dish is *caldeirada*, made with a mélange of fruits from the sea. Fishermen combine the daily catch, perhaps cod, hake, clams, bream, red snapper, squid, crabs, mussels, eel and shrimp, with a few vegetables and seasonings to make a thick and flavorful stew.

3 pounds mixed fish and shellfish, cleaned
3 large onions, peeled and sliced
1-2 garlic cloves, crushed
1/3 cup olive or vegetable oil
3 large tomatoes, peeled and chopped
6 medium-sized potatoes, peeled and sliced thinly
1/2 cup chopped fresh coriander or parsley
salt, pepper to taste
1 cup dry white wine

If the fish is small, leave it whole; otherwise, cut it into serving pieces. Clean the clams and crabs, if used, and crack any shellfish. Sauté the onions and garlic in the oil in a large kettle until tender. Add the tomatoes and cook slowly for 5 minutes. Put the fish, shellfish and potatoes in layers in the kettle. Add the coriander, salt, pepper and wine. Cook slowly until the ingredients are tender, 25 minutes or longer. Serves 8.

MENU

Portuguese Seafood Stew
Cold Cooked Leeks Vinaigrette
Crusty White Bread
Sliced Pineapple au Rhum

Caribbean Chicken Sancocho

In the Spanish-speaking Caribbean islands a popular stew is *sancocho*, made with a variety of meats and vegetables. Most often such favorite foods as yams, dasheens, cassavas, plantains, pineapples and coconuts are among the ingredients. The resulting flavor is most appealing. This version, made with food generally available in the United States, is a good summer buffet dish.

1 pound boneless pork or ham, cut into small cubes
1/2 pound salt pork, diced

1/4 cup (about) vegetable oil
2 frying chickens, about 2½ pounds each, cut up
2 large onions, peeled and sliced
2 garlic cloves, crushed
4 medium-sized tomatoes, peeled, seeded and chopped
2 cups chicken broth
1 bay leaf
1/2 teaspoon dried oregano
3 parsley sprigs
salt, pepper to taste
2 pounds sweet potatoes, peeled and cubed
4 medium-sized carrots, scraped and cut into 1½-inch pieces
2 pounds yellow squash, washed, stemmed and cubed
1/4 cup chopped fresh coriander or parsley

Put the pork or ham, salt pork and oil in a large kettle and sauté until most of the fat is released from the salt pork. Push aside or remove from the kettle. Dry the chicken pieces and sauté a few at a time until golden. Add more oil, if needed. Remove with tongs to a plate. Add the onions and garlic to the drippings and sauté until tender. Add the tomatoes and cook 1 minute. Return the meat and chicken pieces to the kettle. Add the broth, bay leaf, oregano, parsley, salt and pepper and bring to a boil. Lower the heat, cover and cook slowly for 15 minutes. Add the sweet potatoes and carrots. Cook another 15 minutes and add the squash. Continue cooking about 20 minutes longer or until the ingredients are tender. Mix in the coriander. Remove and discard the bay leaf before serving. Serves 10.

MENU

Caribbean Chicken Sancocho
Orange-Cucumber Salad
Warm Corn Muffins
Pineapple Sherbet
Macaroons

French Boeuf Bourguignon

This famous beef stew is cooked *à la bourguignonne*, or "in the style of Burgundy," one of France's great wine producing regions. It is richly flavored with wine and includes small white onions and whole mushrooms, as well as superb garnishes.

5 pounds boneless stewing beef, (chuck, rump, top or
    bottom round), cut into 1½-inch cubes
1/2 cup diced bacon or salt pork
6 tablespoons (about) olive or vegetable oil
2 carrots, scraped and diced
2 medium-sized onions, peeled and chopped
3 tablespoons flour
3-4 garlic cloves, crushed
2 bay leaves
4 parsley sprigs
1 teaspoon dried thyme
3 cups (about) dry red wine
2 cups beef stock or bouillon
salt, pepper to taste
24 small white onions, peeled
6 tablespoons (about) butter or margarine
24 fresh mushrooms, cleaned
2 tablespoons tomato paste

Dry the beef cubes. Heat the bacon or pork and oil in a large kettle and add the beef, a few cubes at a time, to brown on all sides. Remove to a plate. Add the carrots and onions to the drippings and sauté for 5 minutes. Return the beef to the kettle. Sprinkle with the flour and mix. Add the garlic, bay leaves, parsley, thyme, wine and stock. Season with salt and pepper. Bring to a boil. Lower the heat, cover and cook slowly for about 2 hours or until the meat is tender. Add more wine during the cooking, if needed, but there should not be too much liquid. While the stew is cooking, sauté the onions in 3 tablespoons of butter in a saucepan until golden, a minute or two. Add water to cover and cook, covered, until just tender, about 12 minutes. Cut the mushrooms in half length-wise and sauté in the remaining butter, adding more if needed, in a skillet for 4 minutes. Ten minutes before the stew is finished cooking add the tomato paste and stir well. Add the onions and mushrooms, with the drippings, just before taking the dish off the heat. Serves 12.

MENU

French Boeuf Bourguignon
Mixed Green Salad
Crusty French Bread
French Pastry or Cheese Plate

West African Jollof

In the small West African coastal countries bordering the Atlantic, a typical stew called *jollof* is made with chicken or meat, or both, rice and native hot seasonings. Generally it is prepared in very large quantities and served at such celebra-tions as weddings and birthdays. This version of *jollof* can be made even spicier with the addition of more red pepper, if desired.

1/2 pound salt pork, diced
3 tablespoons (about) peanut or vegetable oil
1 pound boneless beef chuck or round,
cut into 1½-inch cubes
2 frying chickens, about 2½ pounds each, cut up
3 large onions, peeled and sliced thinly
4 large tomatoes, peeled and chopped
2 large green peppers, cleaned and cut into strips
2 bay leaves
1-2 teaspoons crushed red peppers
1/2 teaspoon dried thyme
salt, pepper to taste
2 cans (6 ounces each) tomato paste

1 cup water
1 tablespoon fresh lemon juice
2 cups chicken broth
2 cups long grain rice

Put the salt pork and oil in a large kettle and cook until most of the fat is released from the pork. Add the beef cubes, a few at a time, and brown on all sides. Remove to a plate or push aside. Dry the chicken pieces and sauté a few at a time until golden on all sides. Add more oil, if needed. With tongs remove to a plate. Add the onions and sauté until tender. Stir in the tomatoes and green peppers, and more oil, if needed, and sauté 2 minutes. Add the bay leaves, red peppers, thyme, salt, pepper, tomato paste, water and lemon juice and mix well. Cook 1 minute. Return the beef and chicken to the kettle and pour in the chicken broth. Bring to a boil. Lower the heat, cover and cook slowly for 30 minutes. Add the rice and continue to cook slowly, covered, for about 30 minutes, or until the chicken is tender and almost all the liquid has been absorbed by the rice. Serves 10.

Note: Traditional accompaniments for the stew are boiled cabbage or spinach.

MENU

West African Jollof
Mixed Green Salad
Dark Bread
Coconut Pie or Cake

Greek Beef Stifado

In Greek restaurants, it is a premeal custom to visit the kitchen and peer into the pots before ordering. Among the aromatic selections, one customarily will find *stifado*, a well-flavored stew that has been slowly simmered for a long time. This is an excellent dish for an outdoor buffet.

1 cup (about) olive or vegetable oil
4 pounds boneless beef chuck or stew meat,
cut into 1-inch cubes
4 pounds small white onions, peeled
1 can (6 ounces) tomato paste
1½ cups dry red wine
3-4 garlic cloves, peeled and halved
2 sticks cinnamon or 1½ tablespoons ground cinnamon
6 whole cloves
2 bay leaves
salt, pepper to taste

Heat 1/2 cup of the oil in a large kettle. Dry the beef cubes and brown a few pieces at a time in the oil, adding more if needed. Take off·the heat and set aside. Sauté the onions in the remaining heated oil in a skillet until golden on all sides. Spoon, with the drippings, over the meat. Do not mix together. Combine the tomato paste and red wine and pour over the meat and onions. Add the remaining ingredients. Cook very slowly, tightly covered, 2½ to 3 hours, or until the meat is tender. During the cooking check now and then to see if the meat is sticking to the kettle. If so, add a little water. The final sauce, however, should be quite thick and will be better if cooked very slowly. Discard the garlic, cinnamon sticks, cloves and bay leaves before serving. Serves 12.

MENU

Greek Beef Stifado
Hot Buttered Rice
Sliced Cucumber-Green Pepper Salad
Sesame Seed Bread
Baklava or Fresh Fruit

Moroccan Chicken Tajine

In Morocco any mixture of ingredients cooked in a glazed earthenware casserole called a *tajine* has the same name.

There are many variations, each including exotic native foods. Although this one is traditionally made with pickled lemons that must be prepared several days beforehand, ordinary fresh lemons are used in this recipe. A good dish for a summer luncheon.

1/2 cup (about) olive or vegetable oil
3 medium-sized onions, peeled and sliced thinly
2-3 garlic cloves, crushed
2 teaspoons ground ginger
2 teaspoons powdered coriander
1/4 cup chopped fresh parsley
salt, pepper to taste
2 frying chickens, about 2½ pounds each, cut up
1½ cups chicken broth or water
2 medium-sized lemons, quartered
1 cup pitted green olives

Heat the oil in a large kettle and add the onions and garlic. Sauté until tender. Mix in the spices, parsley, salt and pepper and cook 2-3 minutes. Dry the chicken pieces and add to the spice mixture. Fry a few pieces at a time until golden on all sides, adding more oil, if needed. Add the broth or water, cover and cook slowly for 30 minutes. Mix in the lemons and olives and continue to cook slowly for another 20 minutes or until the ingredients are tender. Serves 6.

MENU

Moroccan Chicken Tajine
Parsley Boiled Potatoes
Sliced Tomatoes
Crusty White Bread
Canned Figs and Vanilla Ice Cream

Kentucky Burgoo

This famous southern stew has long been served traditionally in Kentucky at all important outdoor gatherings.

Originally made with squirrel and chicken, *burgoo* contains a large number of vegetables. It is cooked outdoors in a large iron kettle and served in tin cups.

4 pounds mixed meat (pork, beef, veal and/or lamb) shanks
1 roasting or stewing chicken, about 4 pounds
1 tablespoon salt
pepper to taste
4 medium-sized potatoes, peeled and cubed
3 carrots, scraped and diced
2 large onions, peeled and chopped
2 cups shredded green cabbage
2 cups fresh or frozen corn kernels
3 medium-sized tomatoes, peeled and diced
1 package (10 ounces) frozen lima beans
1 package (10 ounces) frozen whole okra
2 tablespoons Worcestershire sauce
1 cup diced green pepper

Put the meat shanks and chicken in a large kettle and pour in enough water to just cover them. Season with salt and pepper. Lower the heat, cover and cook slowly for 1½ hours or longer, until the chicken and meat are tender. Remove from the kettle and cut all the meat from the bones. Cut the meat into bite-sized pieces and return to the kettle. Discard any skin and bones. Heat to boiling. Lower the heat and add all the vegetables except the frozen ones and green pepper. Cover and cook slowly for 20 minutes. Add the frozen vegetables, Worcestershire sauce and green pepper and continue cooking until the ingredients are tender. Check the seasoning. Serves 16.

MENU

Kentucky Burgoo
Warm Corn Muffins
Chocolate Frosted Pound Cake or Sponge Cake

Poulet en Cocotte

In France chicken is often cooked *en cocotte* or in a casserole.

**1 roasting chicken, 3½-4 pounds
salt, pepper to taste
4 sprigs fresh tarragon or 1/2 teaspoon dried tarragon
3 tablespoons (about) butter or margarine
2 tablespoons (about) olive or vegetable oil
16 small white onions, peeled
1/2 cup tomato sauce
bouquet garni (1 bay leaf, 1/2 teaspoon dried thyme,
2 parsley sprigs, wrapped in cheesecloth)
16 small new potatoes, peeled
1 pound fresh mushrooms, cleaned
1 package (9 ounces) frozen artichoke hearts**

Wash the chicken and pat dry. Season inside and out with salt and pepper. Put the tarragon in the cavity. Truss the chicken. Heat the butter and oil in a heavy casserole. Add the chicken and brown on all sides, turning carefully with two spoons so the skin is not broken. Remove to a platter or pan. Add the onions to the drippings and more butter, if needed, and sauté them for about 5 minutes, until translucent. Stir in the tomato sauce. Return the chicken to the dish and add the *bouquet garni*. Season with salt and pepper. Cover tightly and cook on the top of the stove for about 1 hour or until the chicken is just tender. Add the onions and potatoes after the dish has been cooking for 30 minutes; add the mushrooms and artichokes after cooking 45 minutes. Take off the heat. Remove the chicken from the pan and carve it. Serve surrounded with the vegetables. Serves 4.

MENU

*Poulet en Cocotte
Romaine Lettuce Salad
Crusty White Bread
Chocolate or Strawberry Mousse*

Persian Lamb-Vegetable Khoreshe

In Persian cookery a *khoreshe* is a stew made with meat or chicken, fresh or dried vegetables, and spices. Sometimes fruits are added. This adaptation is a good dish for a summer dinner.

1 large eggplant, about 1½ pounds, stemmed and washed
salt
olive or vegetable oil
2 large onions, peeled and sliced
2 pounds boneless lamb, cut into 1-inch cubes
2 large tomatoes, peeled and chopped
2 tablespoons fresh lemon juice
1 teaspoon ground cinnamon
1/2 teaspoon ground nutmeg
pepper to taste

Slice the unpeeled eggplant and put in a colander or strainer. Sprinkle with salt and leave to drain for 30 minutes. Pat dry and set aside. Heat 1/4 cup of oil in a skillet and sauté the eggplant slices, several at a time, until just tender. Add more oil as needed. As they are cooked, remove them to a plate and set aside. Heat 1/4 cup of oil in a large kettle and add the onions. Sauté until tender. Push aside and add the lamb cubes. Brown on all sides. Cover and cook slowly for 20 minutes. Add the sautéed eggplant, tomatoes, lemon juice, cinnamon and nutmeg. Season with salt and pepper and add 1/2 cup water. Cover and cook slowly for about 1 hour or until the ingredients are cooked. Check occasionally to see if a little more water is needed. Serves 6.

MENU

Persian Lamb-Vegetable Khoreshe
Buttered Rice
Mixed Green Salad
Crusty Dark Bread
Vanilla Ice Cream with Chopped Fresh Peaches

Corsican Lamb Stufatu

In Corsica, a lovely French island, there are a number of hearty meat stews, enriched with local seasonings, that are called *stufatus*. This variation also includes macaroni and mushrooms. A good winter dinner dish.

**3 pounds boneless lamb shoulder, cut into
1½-inch cubes
salt, pepper to taste
1/3 cup (about) olive or vegetable oil
2 pounds small white onions, peeled
2-3 garlic cloves, crushed
2 medium-sized tomatoes, peeled and chopped
1½ cups dry white wine
1/2 teaspoon dried basil
8 ounces elbow macaroni or twists
2 cups sliced mushrooms
2 tablespoons butter or margarine
2 tablespoons fresh lemon juice
1/3 cup chopped fresh parsley**

Cut off and discard any excess fat from the lamb. Wipe dry and season with salt and pepper. Heat the oil in a large kettle and brown the lamb, a few pieces at a time, on all sides. Push aside and add the onions and garlic. Sauté until tender. Add the tomatoes, wine and basil. Season with salt and pepper. Bring to a boil. Lower the heat, cover and cook slowly for 1 hour or until the meat and onions are tender. Meanwhile cook the macaroni in boiling salted water until just tender; drain. Sauté the mushrooms in the butter and lemon juice for 3 minutes. Add the mushrooms, macaroni and parsley to the lamb mixture. Cook slowly 5 minutes longer. Serves 8 to 10.

MENU

*Corsican Lamb Stufatu
Artichoke Heart-Lettuce Salad*

Crusty White Bread
Cream Puffs or Eclairs

Sweet-Sour Short Ribs With Noodles

This German-inspired stew is inexpensive and hearty, and makes a good dish for a weekday dinner.

4 pounds beef short ribs, cut into 3-inch pieces
flour
salt, pepper to taste
3 tablespoons shortening or vegetable oil
1 large onion, peeled and sliced
1 cup beef bouillon or water
1/4 cup wine vinegar
3 tablespoons brown sugar
1/2 cup catsup
1/4 cup soy sauce
2 cups fine egg noodles, cooked and drained
1½ cups frozen green peas

Dredge the short ribs with flour seasoned with salt and pepper. Leave on a plate. Heat the shortening in a kettle and sauté the onions in it until tender. Push aside and add the short ribs, a few at a time, to brown on all sides. Pour in the bouillon and bring to a boil. Lower the heat, cover and cook slowly for 1½ hours. Take off the stove and let cool. Skim off any accumulated fat from the top. Add the vinegar, brown sugar, catsup and soy sauce. Mix well. Return to the stove and cook another 30 minutes or until the meat is tender. Mix in the cooked noodles and peas during the last 7 minutes of cooking. Serves 4.

MENU

Sweet-Sour Short Ribs With Noodles
Cabbage-Carrot Salad

Warm Dark Rolls
Baked Apples

Costa Brava Seafood Stew

Zarzuela de mariscos is a very popular stew along the Spanish Mediterranean coast. Its name, which means "musical comedy of seafood," is said to have derived from a seventeenth century performance given at the palace of King Philip IV, La Zarzuela. This particular version is good for a summer lunch.

**2 pounds mixed white-fleshed fish (halibut, bass,
red snapper, flounder, haddock), cut in chunks
2 small squid, cleaned and cut up
flour
1/2 cup (about) olive oil
24 large shrimp, shelled and deveined
1 large onion, peeled and chopped
1-2 garlic cloves, minced
3 large tomatoes, peeled and chopped
1 bay leaf
salt, pepper to taste
dry white wine
1 can pimiento, chopped
1/3 cup chopped fresh parsley
2 tablespoons brandy or Pernod**

Dust the fish and squid with flour. Heat the oil in a kettle and fry the seafood in it on both sides until golden. Remove to a warm platter. Add the shrimp and sauté in the drippings until pink. Add more oil, if needed. Remove to a platter. Add the onion and garlic to the drippings and sauté until tender. Mix in the tomatoes and bay leaf and cook for 2 minutes. Return the fish, squid and shrimp to the kettle. Season with salt and pepper. Add white wine to cover. Cook over moderate heat about 10 minutes, or until the ingredients are tender. Add the pimiento, parsley and brandy. Cook another minute or two. Serves 6.

MENU

Costa Brava Seafood Stew
Buttered Rice
Mixed Green Salad
Crusty White Bread
Fresh Peach Tart

New England Boiled Dinner

Although not exactly a stew in the true sense, this traditional New England one-pot meal has long been a treasured dish. It is easy to prepare and can be reheated.

4-5 pounds corned beef brisket
6 carrots, scraped
6 medium-sized onions, peeled
6 medium-sized potatoes, peeled
2 medium-sized white turnips, pared and quartered
1 head green cabbage, coarsely shredded
6 medium-sized beets, cooked, peeled and kept warm

Wash the beef and put in a kettle. Cover with cold water. Bring to a boil. Lower the heat, cover and cook very slowly for 3-4 hours or until the meat is tender. Add the carrots, onions, potatoes and turnips during the last 30 minutes of cooking. Add the cabbage about 20 minutes before the end of the cooking. To serve, take out the meat and slice. Put in the center of a platter and arrange the cooked vegetables around it. Serve the beets separately. Serves 6.

MENU

New England Boiled Dinner
Warm Parkerhouse Rolls
Apple Pie

Dutch Hutspot

The Dutch version of hotchpotch or thick stew traditionally is made with beef and a few humble vegetables. It is eaten throughout the year but particularly to celebrate the end of the Spanish siege of Leyden in 1574, when the starving population was given *hutspot*. It is a good winter supper dish.

2 pounds beef chuck or flank
1 teaspoon salt
1½ pounds carrots, scraped and sliced
2 pounds (about 6 medium-sized) potatoes,
peeled and quartered
2 large onions, peeled and chopped
2 tablespoons light cream or milk
2 tablespoons butter or margarine
salt, pepper to taste

Cut any fat from the beef and, if the flank is used, take off any membranes. Put in a large saucepan with the salt and 4 cups of water. Bring to a boil. Remove any scum that rises to the top. Lower the heat, cover and simmer about 1½ hours. Add the carrots, potatoes and onions and simmer another hour, or until the vegetables are tender. Remove the meat to a warm platter and cut into strips. If flank is used it should be cut across the grain. Take out the vegetables and mash with the cream, butter, salt and pepper. Add some of the broth to thin the mixture, if desired. To serve, spoon the vegetables onto a platter and surround with the meat slices. Serves 6.

MENU

Dutch Hutspot
Cole Slaw
Warm Dark Rolls
Rice or Berry Pudding

Spanish Bean-Sausage Stew

This savory stew, called *fabada a la Asturiana*, is one of Spain's great dishes. It is from the northwest region of Asturias along the Bay of Biscay, and its name derives from the local large white bean, *fabe*, a traditional ingredient in the stew. Because the native sausages and pork products are not easily obtainable outside of Spain, this dish is an adaptation of the original.

2 pounds large white beans, washed and drained
6 cups water
3 large onions, peeled and coarsely chopped
3 garlic cloves, crushed
6 tablespoons olive or vegetable oil
2 cans (6 ounces each) tomato paste
salt, pepper to taste
1 pound smoked bacon in one piece
8 smoked ham hocks
1 pound blood sausage (optional)
1 pound *chorizo* (Spanish sausage) or other garlic sausage,
sliced and cooked
1/4 teaspoon ground saffron,
previously soaked in hot water

Cover the beans with water in a kettle and bring to a boil. Boil for 2 minutes. Remove from the heat. Cover and let stand for 1 hour. Meanwhile, sauté the onions and garlic in the olive oil in a large casserole or heavy kettle until tender. Stir in the tomato paste and season with salt and pepper. When the beans are done, put them, with their liquid, in the casserole or kettle over the onions. Mix well. Add the bacon. Pour in enough water to completely cover the ingredients. Bring to a boil. Lower the heat, cover tightly and cook as slowly as possible for 1 hour. Add the ham hocks and blood sausage and continue cooking slowly for about 1 hour longer or until the ingredients are cooked. Add the *chorizo* and saffron 30 minutes before the dish is finished cooking. Add more water while cooking, if needed. Serves 8 to 10.

MENU

Spanish Bean-Sausage Stew
Warm Corn Bread
Sliced Fresh or Canned Pineapple

Daube de Boeuf

This French country stew takes its name from the earthen-ware pot, or *daubière*, in which it is cooked. It may also be prepared in a kettle, and makes an excellent dish for company.

3 pounds lean stewing beef (rump, chuck, top or
bottom round), cut into 2-inch cubes
1 cup dry white or red wine
1/4 cup brandy
1/2 cup olive or vegetable oil
2 large onions, peeled and sliced thinly
4 carrots, scraped and diced
2 bay leaves
1 teaspoon dried thyme
1/4 cup chopped fresh parsley
salt, freshly ground pepper to taste
1/2 cup diced thick bacon
2 garlic cloves, crushed
3 medium-sized tomatoes, peeled, seeded and chopped
1 cup sliced fresh mushrooms
1 small strip orange peel
1/2 teaspoon dried rosemary
12 pitted black olives

Put the beef cubes, wine, brandy, 1/4 cup olive oil, 1 sliced onion, 2 diced carrots, bay leaves, thyme and 2 tablespoons parsley in a large bowl. Season with salt and pepper; marinate about 2½ hours. Stir the ingredients now and then. When ready to cook, put the bacon, garlic, remaining 2 tablespoons of oil, 1 sliced onion and 2 diced carrots in a kettle and sauté for 5 minutes. Take the meat from the marinade and wipe dry. Reserve the marinade. Brown a few pieces at a time in the oil drippings, pushing the vegetables aside. When all the meat is browned mix in the tomatoes, mushrooms, orange peel and rosemary. Season with salt and pepper. Pour in the reserved marinade, including the vegetables, cover and cook slowly for 1 hour. Stir in the olives after cooking for 30 minutes. When the cooking is finished, add the remaining parsley. Remove and discard the bay leaves. Serves 8 to 10.

MENU

Daube de Boeuf
Boiled Potatoes or Rice
Mixed Green Salad
French Bread
Cheese Plate

San Francisco Cioppino

This marvelous seafood stew is believed to have been created in San Francisco, but nobody knows how it got the name *cioppino*. Some people suspect that Italian or perhaps Portuguese fishermen first prepared *cioppino*, since it resembles stews of the Mediterranean. At any rate, restaurants along Fishermen's Wharf started serving it about 1900, and it has been a treasured specialty in California ever since. This is one of many variations. A good late supper dish.

1 large onion, peeled and chopped
2-3 garlic cloves, crushed
1 medium-sized green pepper, seeded and diced
1/3 cup olive or vegetable oil
2 cans (1 pound each) tomatoes
1 can (8 ounces) tomato sauce
1 bay leaf
1/4 teaspoon dried oregano, thyme, rosemary or basil
or 1/8 teaspoon of two of them

salt, pepper to taste
2 pounds firm fish (bass, halibut, cod, rock, haddock)
1 large Dungeness crab or lobster
1 dozen fresh clams in shells
1 pound large shrimp in shells
2 cups (about) dry white or red wine

Sauté the onion, garlic and green pepper in the oil in a large kettle until tender. Add the tomatoes, tomato sauce, bay leaf, herbs, salt and pepper and bring to a boil. Lower the heat, cover and simmer slowly for 1 hour. While the sauce is cooking, cut the fish into serving pieces. Clean and crack the crab or lobster and put the pieces in a large kettle. Scrub the clams to remove any dirt. Cut the shrimp shells down the backs and remove any black veins. Place the clams and shrimp both over the crabs. Add the fish and then pour the sauce over the seafood. Add the wine. Cover and cook slowly, 20-30 minutes, or until the clams open and the seafood is cooked. Add more wine while cooking, if needed. Discard the bay leaf. Serves 6.

MENU

San Francisco Cioppino
Warm Sourdough or French Bread
Strawberry Ice Cream Pie

South American Estofado

In the various South American cuisines there are several versions of interesting stews called *estofados*. Of European origin, they differ in that the ingredients include such American foods as corn and sweet potatoes.

1 large onion, peeled and chopped
3 tablespoons vegetable oil
2 pounds stew beef, cut into 1½-inch cubes
beef bouillon
salt, pepper to taste

6 small sweet potatoes, peeled
6 medium-sized white potatoes, peeled
4 carrots, scraped
2 cups fresh or frozen corn kernels
1 medium-sized green pepper, seeded and chopped
2 tablespoons chopped fresh parsley
1/8 teaspoon cayenne pepper

Sauté the onion in the oil in a large kettle until tender. Push aside and add the beef, several cubes at a time, to brown on all sides. Add the bouillon to cover, salt and pepper, cover and cook slowly for 1 hour. Add the vegetables, except the green pepper, and more bouillon, if needed. Cook slowly, covered, for about 30 minutes longer, or until the ingredients are cooked. Add the green pepper, parsley and cayenne 5 minutes before the cooking is finished. Serves 8.

MENU

South American Estofado
Sliced Cucumbers and Tomatoes Vinaigrette
Warm Corn Bread
Banana Cream Pie

Moroccan Lamb Couscous

In Morocco and other North African countries, a *couscous* is a favorite hearty stew made with a grain of the same name, vegetables, meat or poultry. The grain is sold in the United States at supermarkets or specialty food stores. Traditionally the stew is cooked in a *couscoussière*, a sort of double boiler with a perforated top pot placed over a kettle.

1 cup chickpeas
1 package (500 grams or 17 ounces) *couscous*
3 pounds lean lamb, leg or shoulder, cut into large cubes
1/3 cup (about) olive or vegetable oil

2 large onions, peeled and chopped
1 can (6 ounces) tomato paste
1 teaspoon ground red pepper
1/2 teaspoon ground cumin
salt, pepper to taste
10 cups water or meat broth
3 carrots, scraped and sliced thickly
2 large zucchini, washed and sliced thickly
2 medium-sized turnips, peeled and cut into large cubes
1 large green pepper, seeded and cut into strips
1/2 cup chopped fresh coriander or parsley

Soak the chickpeas in water to cover overnight. Spread the *couscous* on a large tray or platter and sprinkle with enough water to dampen. Mix about with the hands. Brown the lamb cubes, several pieces at a time, in the oil in a *couscoussière*, soup pan or Dutch oven. Remove to a plate. Add the onions to the drippings and sauté until tender. Stir in the tomato paste, red pepper, cumin, salt and pepper. Add the water or broth and bring to a boil. Return the lamb to the kettle. Add the chickpeas and lower the heat. Cook slowly, covered, for 30 minutes. Add the carrots, zucchini, turnips and green pepper to the stew. Put the *couscous* in the top of the cooker, or in a colander lined with cheesecloth, and place over the kettle. Cover and continue cooking for about 30 minutes longer, or until the *couscous* and stew ingredients are cooked. Stir in the coriander or parsley. To serve, spoon the *couscous* onto a large platter and arrange the lamb and vegetables around it. Sprinkle some of the chickpeas and liquid over the top as a garnish. Serves 8.
Note: Canned chickpeas can be used, if desired. If so, it will not be necessary to soak them overnight.

MENU

Moroccan Lamb Couscous
Fresh Fruit Compote

Country Fish-Vegetable Stew

A nourishing stew that can be easily made with fresh or frozen codfish fillets.

4 medium-sized potatoes, pared and cubed
3 carrots, scraped and sliced
2 cups cut-up green beans
3 medium-sized onions, peeled and quartered
salt, pepper to taste
1½ pounds codfish fillets, cut up
2 tablespoons butter or margarine, softened
2 tablespoons flour
1/3 cup chopped fresh parsley

Put the potatoes, carrots, green beans and onions in a soup pan or Dutch oven. Add enough water to cover them. Season with salt and pepper. Cover and cook slowly for 15 minutes. Add the codfish and a little more water and continue to cook slowly for about 10 minutes or until the ingredients are tender. Combine the softened butter and flour and form into tiny balls. Drop into the stew and cook slowly, stirring, until thickened. Stir in the parsley. Serves 4.

MENU

Country Fish-Vegetable Stew
Buttered Toasted English Muffins
Warm Apple Pie

Grecian Lamb-Artichoke Stew

The Greeks are devoted to a stew made with an interesting combination of lamb and artichokes which is flavored with fresh lemon juice.

1/4 cup olive or vegetable oil
1 large onion, peeled and chopped

3 pounds shoulder of lamb, cut up
2 tablespoons flour
3 cups water
juice of 2 lemons
salt, pepper to taste
2 packages (9 ounces each) frozen artichoke hearts,
defrosted
2 eggs

Heat the oil in a large skillet. Add the onion and sauté until tender. Wipe the lamb dry and brown on all sides in the drippings. Sprinkle with the flour and mix well. Add the water, juice of 1 lemon, salt and pepper and cook slowly, covered, for 45 minutes. Add the artichokes and cook until tender, about 15 minutes. Remove from the heat. Beat the eggs until creamy. Stir in the remaining lemon juice. Slowly add some of the hot stew liquid. Mix well and return to the stew. Cook over low heat, mixing well, until the sauce thickens. Do not boil. Remove from the heat and serve at once. Serves 6 to 8.

MENU

Grecian Lamb-Artichoke Stew
Sesame Seed Bread
Baklava or Honeyed Walnut Cake

Napoleon's Poulet Marengo

This popular dish was created by Napoleon's chef, Dunand, after the French won an outstanding victory against the Austrians in the northern town of Marengo in 1800.

2 frying chickens, about 2½ pounds each, cut up
salt, pepper to taste
6 tablespoons olive oil
3 tablespoons butter or margarine
1 pound fresh mushrooms, cleaned and dried
2 garlic cloves

1 cup chopped onions
1/3 cup tomato purée
1 cup dry white wine
4 medium-sized tomatoes, peeled, seeded, chopped
bouquet garni **(bay leaf, sprig of parsley,**
1/4 teaspoon thyme)

Wash the chicken pieces and wip dry. Season with salt and pepper. Heat the oil and butter in a large heavy casserole. Add the chicken pieces and fry until golden on all sides. Remove to a warm platter. Carefully pull the stems from one half pound of the mushrooms. Reserve the caps. Slice the stems and the other half pound of mushrooms. Sauté in the drippings for 4 minutes. With a slotted spoon remove to a plate. Add the garlic and onions to the drippings and sauté until tender. Stir in the tomato purée and wine. Bring to a boil. Cook over fairly high heat for 5 minutes. Return the chicken pieces to the kettle. Add the tomatoes, *bouquet garni* and season with salt and pepper. Cook slowly, covered, for about 35 minutes, or until the chicken is tender. Add the reserved sautéed sliced mushrooms and mushroom caps 10 minutes before the cooking is finished. Remove and discard the bay leaf and parsley. To serve, arrange the chicken pieces on a large platter. Spoon the tomato sauce and sliced mushrooms over them. Top with the mushroom caps. Serves 8.

MENU

Napoleon's Poulet Marengo
Buttered Crusty French Bread
French Pastries

Japanese Sukiyaki

This popular Japanese dish is an excellent company meal that can be made in front of guests, in the kitchen or outdoors, if desired. An electric skillet, special sukiyaki pan or ordinary skillet can be used.

1¼ cups soy sauce
1¼ cups *sake* or dry white wine
1/3 cup sugar
1½ teaspoons monosodium glutamate
1 cup (about) vegetable oil
3 pounds beef sirloin, thinly sliced
3 medium-sized onions, peeled and thinly sliced
8 green onions, cut into 3-inch lengths
1/2 pound fresh mushrooms, cleaned and sliced
1 cup sliced bamboo shoots

Combine the soy sauce, *sake*, sugar and monosodium glutamate. Pour into a pitcher and set aside. Add enough oil to
grease a sukiyaki cooker or skillet. With chopsticks or a fork,
dip the meat slices, a few at a time, into the soy-*sake* mixture
and spread over the surface of the skillet. Brown and push
aside. Add the vegetables, a few at a time, and a generous
portion of the soy-*sake* mixture. Cook, turning until just tender. Do not overcook as the vegetables should be just tender
or a little crisp. Serves 8.
*Note: When cooking in front of guests arrange all the ingredients
attractively on bamboo dishes or platters and place near the cooking utensils. Cook slowly, being careful not to overload the utensil
with too many ingredients.*

MENU

Japanese Sukiyaki
Steamed Rice
Crisp Crackers
Fruit-Topped Lemon Sherbet

Southern Chicken and Okra Stew

A good Sunday dinner dish.

1 frying chicken, about 3 pounds, cut up
3 tablespoons butter or margarine

1 tablespoon olive or vegetable oil
1 large onion, peeled and chopped
2 tablespoons tomato paste
1/2 cup (about) water
1/2 teaspoon dried oregano
salt, pepper to taste
2 packages (10 ounces each) frozen okra, defrosted,
   or fresh okra, if available
juice of 1/2 lemon

Wash the chicken pieces and wipe dry. Melt the butter with the oil in a large skillet and fry the chicken on all sides until golden. Cover and cook over low heat for 15 minutes. Remove the chicken to a plate. Add the onion to the drippings and sauté until tender. Stir in the tomato paste, water, oregano, salt and pepper and mix well. Return the chicken to the kettle. Add the okra. Cook slowly, covered, about 20 minutes, until the chicken and okra are tender. Add a little more water while cooking, if needed. Mix in the lemon juice and serve. Serves 4.

MENU

Southern Chicken and Okra Stew
Warm Corn Sticks
Peach-Vanilla Ice Cream Coupes

Portuguese Pork-Clam Stew

An unusual combination that was created by Portuguese fishermen with their favorite meat and one of their best seafoods.

2 pounds lean boneless pork, cut into small cubes
1/4 cup (about) olive or vegetable oil
2 large onions, peeled and sliced
1-2 garlic cloves, crushed
4 large tomatoes, peeled and chopped

1 can (6 ounces) tomato paste
dry white wine or water
1/2 teaspoon paprika
salt, pepper to taste
24 hard-shelled clams, scrubbed and washed
1/3 cup chopped fresh parsley

Dry the pork cubes and brown on all sides in the oil in a large skillet. Remove with a slotted spoon. Add the onions to the drippings and more oil, if needed, and sauté until tender. Return the pork to the skillet. Add the tomatoes and sauté 2 or 3 minutes. Stir in the tomato paste. Add enough wine or water to cover the ingredients. Mix in the paprika, salt and pepper. Stir well and bring to a boil. Lower the heat and cook slowly, covered, about 1½ hours, or until the meat is tender. Add more wine during the cooking, if needed. Add the clams about 15 minutes before the cooking is finished, or until the shells open. Mix in the parsley. Serves 4.

MENU

Portuguese Pork-Clam Stew
Crusty White Bread
Orange Custard

Hasenpfeffer

This flavorful German specialty, which means "hare pepper," can be made with rabbit, which is often available frozen in supermarkets, or with chicken.

2 fresh or frozen rabbits (2½-3 pounds each),
cut into serving pieces
equal parts of wine vinegar and water to cover the
rabbit pieces
2 medium-sized onions, peeled and sliced
2 bay leaves
4 juniper berries

4 whole cloves
2 tablespoons sugar
6 peppercorns, bruised
salt and pepper to taste
flour
butter or margarine
1/2 cup sour cream at room temperature

Put the rabbit pieces in a large crock or kettle, and add the vinegar, water, onions, bay leaves, juniper berries, cloves, sugar, peppercorns and salt. Let stand, covered, in a cool place for 2 days. Turn over the rabbit pieces 1 or 2 times daily. When the marinating is finished, take out the rabbit pieces and strain the marinade, reserving it. Dry the rabbit pieces, and dust with flour seasoned with salt and pepper. Fry in butter in a kettle until golden on all sides. Add some of the strained marinade and cook very slowly, covered, until the rabbit is tender, about 1 hour. Add more marinade as needed while cooking. Mix in the sour cream and remove from the stove. Serves 6.

MENU

Hasenpfeffer
Crusty Dark Bread
Warm Apple Strudel

Mediterranean Fish Stew

Serve from a handsome tureen for a company supper or late evening meal.

2 medium-sized onions, peeled and sliced
1-2 garlic cloves, crushed
1/3 cup olive or vegetable oil
1 can (29 ounces) tomatoes
1 large bay leaf
1/2 teaspoon dried basil

3 parsley sprigs
1 cup dry white wine
3 pounds mixed cleaned fish, cut into serving pieces
3 flat anchovy fillets, drained and cut up
pepper to taste
1 pound whole fresh mushrooms, cleaned
3 tablespoons butter or margarine
1 tablespoon fresh lemon juice
1/4 cup chopped fresh parsley
slices of crusty white bread

Sauté the onions and garlic in the oil in a skillet or large saucepan until tender. Add the tomatoes, bay leaf, basil and parsley and cook 5 minutes. Add the wine, fish, anchovies and pepper. Pour in enough water to cover. Cook over fairly high heat until the fish is just tender, about 12 minutes. While the stew is cooking, sauté the mushrooms in the butter and lemon juice for 5 minutes. Add, with the parsley, to the stew. Correct the seasoning. Discard the bay leaf and parsley sprigs. Spoon the fish, mushrooms and broth over the crusty bread slices in large soup bowls. Serves 6 to 8.

MENU

Mediterranean Fish Stew
Warm Garlic Bread
Cheese Plate with Crackers

Pollo alla Cacciatora

Italian chicken cooked in hunter's style, with vegetables, wine and herbs, is a well-known dish that is excellent fare for any dinner.

2 frying chickens, about 2½ pounds each, cut up
salt, pepper to taste
1/4 cup butter or margarine
3 tablespoons (about) olive or vegetable oil

3/4 pound fresh mushrooms, cleaned and sliced
2 medium-sized onions, peeled and sliced
1-2 garlic cloves, crushed
1 can (1 pound, 12 ounces) Italian-style tomatoes
1 cup dry white wine
1/2 teaspoon dried thyme
1/2 teaspoon dried oregano
1/4 cup chopped fresh parsley

Wash the chicken pieces and wipe dry. Season with salt and pepper. Heat the butter and oil in a large kettle. Add the chicken and brown on all sides until golden. Remove to a plate. Add the mushrooms to the drippings and sauté for 4 minutes. With a slotted spoon, remove to a plate. Add the onions and garlic and more oil, if needed. Sauté until the onions are tender. Return the chicken pieces to the kettle. Add the tomatoes, wine, thyme, oregano and season with salt and pepper. Bring to a boil. Lower the heat and cook slowly, covered, about 45 minutes, or until the chicken is tender. Stir in the mushrooms and parsley 5 minutes before the cooking is finished. Serves 8.

MENU

Pollo alla Cacciatora
Bread Sticks
Spumoni Ice Cream

New Zealand Lamb Stew

Some of the world's best lamb is from the small country of New Zealand. It is particularly good in this wine-flavored stew enhanced with vegetables.

4 pounds lamb shoulder, cut into large pieces
1/4 cup (about) vegetable oil
2 medium-sized onions, peeled and sliced
1 garlic clove, crushed

2 carrots, scraped and sliced
2 cups dry red wine
1 teaspoon dried oregano or rosemary
salt, pepper to taste
1 package (10 ounces) frozen green peas
1/2 pound sliced fresh mushrooms
or 1 can (6 ounces) sliced mushrooms, drained

Dry the lamb and brown in the oil on all sides in a large kettle. Remove to a platter. Pour off any excess fat. Add the onions, garlic, carrots and more oil to the kettle, if needed. Sauté 5 minutes. Return the lamb to the kettle. Add the wine, oregano, salt and pepper. Bring to a boil. Lower the heat and cook slowly, covered, about 1¼ hours, or until the lamb is cooked. Add the peas and mushrooms 10 minutes before the cooking is finished. Serves 8.

MENU

New Zealand Lamb Stew
Warm Bran Muffins
Strawberry Chiffon Pie

Azerbaidzhan Spinach-Veal Stew

In Russia's southern republic of Azerbaidzhan cooks have long filled stewpots with the highly seasoned favorite foods found in this recipe.

2 pounds veal or lamb shoulder, cut into 1½-inch cubes
2 tablespoons (about) vegetable oil
1 large onion, peeled and sliced
1/2 cup minced green onions, with tops
1 garlic clove, crushed
1/3 cup tomato paste
2 pounds fresh spinach, cleaned and cut up
water
salt, pepper to taste

1 cup plain yogurt at room temperature
1 tablespoon chopped fresh dill

Trim any excess fat from the meat and wipe dry. Brown on all sides in the oil in a skillet or Dutch oven. Push aside and add the onions, garlic and more oil, if needed. Sauté until tender. Stir in the tomato paste and spinach and mix well. Add water to cover, and season with salt and pepper. Bring to a boil. Lower the heat, cover and cook slowly for about 1¼ hours or until the meat is cooked. Add a little more water, if needed, during the cooking. When done, stir in the yogurt and dill and leave on the stove long enough to heat through. Serves 6.

MENU

Azerbaidzhan Spinach-Veal Stew
Crusty Dark Bread
Raisin-Rice Pudding

Chicken-Vegetable Stew with Pasta

A hearty dish good for a winter meal.

1 stalk celery, chopped
1 carrot, peeled and chopped
1 medium-sized onion, peeled and chopped
1/4 cup olive or vegetable oil
1 teaspoon paprika
8 chicken thighs (about 2 pounds)
1 can (1 pound) tomatoes
3 cups cut-up fresh vegetables
1 tablespoon fresh lemon juice
salt, pepper to taste
2 cups pasta (spaghettini, macaroni or noodles)
1/2 cup chopped fresh parsley
1-2 teaspoons seeded and crushed red peppers
(optional)

Sauté the celery, carrot, and onion in the oil in a large skillet until tender. Stir in the paprika and cook 1 minute. Dry the chicken thighs and brown until golden on all sides. Add the tomatoes, vegetables, lemon juice, salt and pepper. Cook slowly, covered, for 30 minutes, or until the chicken is cooked. Meanwhile, cook the pasta and drain. Add, with the parsley and peppers, to the chicken mixture and cook another 5 minutes. Serves 4.

MENU

Chicken-Vegetable Stew with Pasta
Wheat Crackers
Chocolate Ice Cream with Grated Coconut

Budapest Beef Goulash

This is a Hungarian goulash that would be excellent for an evening get-together.

2 pounds boneless beef chuck or stew meat,
cut into 1½-inch cubes
2 tablespoons (about) lard or shortening
2 large onions, peeled and chopped
2-3 tablespoons paprika
salt, pepper to taste
2 medium-sized tomatoes, peeled and chopped
1 pound (3 medium-sized) potatoes, peeled and chopped

Wipe the meat cubes dry. Brown a few pieces at a time on all sides in lard in a skillet or large saucepan. Push aside and add the onions and more lard, if needed. Sauté until tender. Stir in the paprika and cook 1 minute. Season with salt and pepper. Add enough water to cover and cook very slowly, tightly covered, for 1 hour. Add the tomatoes and potatoes. Continue to cook another 30 minutes, or until the beef and potatoes are tender. Add a little more water during the cooking, if needed. Serves 4 to 6.

MENU

Budapest Beef Goulash
Pumpernickel
Chocolate-Garnished Cream Puffs

Lemony Veal Stew

This stew is elegant as a main course.

2 pounds boneless veal, cut into 1½-inch cubes
flour
salt, pepper to taste
2 large carrots, scraped and diced
2 large onions, peeled and chopped
3 tablespoons (about) butter or margarine
4 medium-sized potatoes, peeled and cubed
2 teaspoons grated lemon rind
juice of 2 lemons
pinch of nutmeg

Dry the veal cubes and dredge in flour seasoned with salt and pepper. In a skillet sauté the carrots and onions in the butter for 5 minutes. Push aside, add the floured veal cubes, and brown on all sides. Add more butter, if needed. Add water to cover and cook slowly, covered, for 1½ hours. Add the potatoes and continue to cook slowly for 20 minutes, or until the ingredients are cooked. Add more water during the cooking, if needed. Stir in the lemon rind, lemon juice and nutmeg. Cook another 5 minutes. Serves 4 to 6.

MENU

Lemony Veal Stew
Warm White Rolls
Cold Chocolate Soufflé

Spanish Chicken Chilindron

In Spain dishes that are cooked in a flavorful sauce of onions, garlic, tomatoes, ham and peppers are called *chilindron*. They are from the region of Aragon.

1 frying chicken, 3-3½ pounds, cut up
salt, pepper to taste
1/3 cup olive or vegetable oil
1 large onion, peeled and sliced
1 garlic clove, minced
3 small red or green peppers, seeded and minced
1/4 pound smoked ham, diced
4 large tomatoes, peeled and chopped
2 canned pimientos, chopped
12 pitted black or green olives

Wash and dry the chicken pieces. Season with salt and pepper. Fry in the heated oil in a skillet until golden on all sides. Remove to a plate. Add the onion, garlic, peppers and ham to the drippings and sauté for 5 minutes. Add the tomatoes and pimientos and cook over medium heat for 5 minutes. Return the chicken pieces to the kettle. Season with salt and pepper. Cover tightly and cook over very low heat about 30 minutes. Add a little water while cooking, if needed. Stir in the olives shortly before serving. Serves 4.

MENU

Spanish Chicken Chilindron
Warm Garlic Bread
Orange Cream Pie

Beer Beef Stew

A good dish for a Saturday night supper.

2 pounds beef chuck or stew meat,
cut into 1½-inch cubes
3 tablespoons (about) shortening
2 large onions, peeled and sliced
2 tablespoons flour
salt, pepper to taste
2 teaspoons sugar
1/2 teaspoon dried thyme or basil
1 cup (about) beer
1/2 cup beef bouillon or water
4 carrots, scraped and cut up
4 medium-sized potatoes, peeled and cubed

Dry the beef and brown in the shortening in a Dutch oven. Push aside and add the onions. Sauté until tender. Sprinkle in the flour and season with salt and pepper. Add the sugar, thyme, beer and bouillon and simmer, covered, for 1 hour. Add the carrots and potatoes and continue cooking for about 30 minutes longer, or until the ingredients are cooked. Add a little more beer during the cooking, if needed. Serves 6.

MENU

Beer Beef Stew
Rye Bread
Warm Apple Pie

Daube of Duckling

Here is another good French *daube* dish that could be served for a holiday or special occasion dinner.

1 duckling, 4-5 pounds, cut up
1 cup dry white wine
1/4 cup brandy (optional)
7 tablespoons (about) olive or vegetable oil
1 garlic clove, minced
1 large bay leaf, crumbled

1/2 teaspoon dried thyme
6 parsley sprigs
salt, pepper to taste
1/2 cup diced smoked ham
1 large onion, peeled and sliced
3 carrots, scraped and sliced thinly
4 medium-sized tomatoes, peeled and chopped
1 cup whole small mushrooms, cleaned
12 pitted black olives

Wash the duckling pieces and wipe dry. Place in a large shallow dish or crock. Add the wine, brandy, 1/4 cup oil, garlic, bay leaf, thyme, parsley, salt and pepper. Marinate 3-4 hours. Turn over the duckling a few times. When ready to cook, put the ham, 3 tablespoons oil, the onion and carrots in a large skillet or saucepan and sauté for 5 minutes. With a slotted spoon remove the ham and vegetables to a plate. Take the duckling pieces from the marinade and wipe dry. Reserve the marinade. Fry the duckling on all sides in the drippings, adding more oil if needed. Lower the heat, cover and cook over a medium flame, for about 20 minutes, or until most of the grease from the duckling has been released. Spoon off the grease and discard. Return the ham and sautéed vegetables to the dish. Add the tomatoes and marinade. Cook slowly, covered, about 1 hour, or until the duckling is tender. Add the mushrooms and olives 15 minutes before the cooking is finished. Serves 4.

MENU

Daube of Duckling
Crusty White Bread
Fruit Tarts

Irish Stew

This is the traditional preparation for a stew that has become very popular in American restaurants.

3 pounds breast of lamb
5 medium-sized onions, peeled and sliced
3 pounds (9 medium sized) potatoes, peeled and sliced
salt, pepper to taste
1 tablespoon chopped fresh parsley

Remove the fat from the lamb and cut into several pieces. In a large saucepan or Dutch oven arrange a layer of the lamb, then a layer of onions and potatoes. Sprinkle each with salt and pepper. Top with the parsley. Add enough water to cover the ingredients. Bring to a boil and remove any scum. Lower the heat, cover and simmer for 2-2½ hours or until the ingredients are well cooked. Add a little more water during the cooking, if needed. Serves 4 to 6.

MENU

Irish Stew
Soda Bread or Buttermilk Biscuits
Fruit Cake

Rumanian Chicken Tocana

This well-flavored dish is typical of the *tocanas*, or stews, prepared in Rumania.

2 frying chickens, about 2½ pounds each, cut up
salt, pepper to taste
2 medium-sized onions, peeled and sliced thinly
2 garlic cloves, crushed
1/3 cup (about) olive or vegetable oil
2 cups dry white wine or chicken broth
1 cup sliced pitted black olives
1/2 cup chopped fresh parsley
1/2 cup sour cream at room temperature

Wash the chicken pieces and wipe dry. Season with salt and pepper. Sauté the onions and garlic in the oil in a large skillet. Add the chicken pieces and brown on all sides. Add the wine and mix well. Cover and cook slowly for 1 hour. Add the olives, parsley and sour cream. Cook another 5 minutes or until the chicken is tender. Serves 6.

MENU

Rumanian Chicken Tocana
Warm Corn Bread
Fruit Compote
Nut Cookies

Meatball-Fruit Stew

This recipe is inspired by the South American fondness for combining beef and fruit in flavorful stews.

2 pounds lean ground beef
1 cup fine dry breadcrumbs
2 eggs
1 teaspoon dried oregano
salt, pepper to taste
3 tablespoons (about) vegetable oil
2 cups drained pineapple cubes
1 medium-sized green pepper, cleaned and chopped
2 cups chopped canned peaches

In a large bowl combine the beef, breadcrumbs, eggs, oregano, salt and pepper. Mix well and shape into 1½-inch balls. In a kettle or saucepan heat the oil and brown the meatballs on all sides in it, adding more oil if needed. Add 1½ cups of water, cover and cook slowly for 30 minutes. Check a few times to see if more water is needed to keep the meatballs from sticking to the pan. Stir in the remaining ingredients and leave on the stove long enough to heat through. Serves 6 to 8.

MENU

Meatball-Fruit Stew
Warm Whole-Wheat Rolls
Coconut Cream Pudding

Turkish Lamb Pilaf

This is one of the many excellent lamb-rice dishes that have been prepared for centuries in Turkish kitchens.

2 medium-sized onions, peeled and chopped
1/4 cup butter or margarine
2 pounds leg or shoulder of lamb, cut into 1-inch cubes
1/4 cup tomato paste
1 cup tomato juice
1/2 teaspoon dried thyme or oregano
salt, pepper to taste
1½ cups uncooked long grain rice
2 cups (about) chicken broth
1/4 cup chopped fresh parsley

In a kettle or large saucepan sauté the onions in the butter until tender. Push aside and add the lamb cubes, several at a time, to brown on all sides. Mix in the tomato paste, tomato juice, thyme, salt and pepper. Cook slowly, covered, for 1 hour. Add a little water during the cooking, if needed. Mix in the rice and chicken broth and continue to cook slowly for about 30 minutes longer, or until the rice is tender and most of the liquid has been absorbed. It may be necessary to add a little more broth during the cooking if the stew becomes too dry. Do not stir during the cooking. Mix in the parsley just before serving. Serves 4 to 6.

MENU

Turkish Lamb Pilaf
Sesame Seed Bread

Fresh Melon
Chocolate Cookies

Flounder-Sauerkraut Smetana Stew

A good fish-sauerkraut dish flavored with herbs and sour cream.

1 large onion, peeled and chopped
1/3 cup minced carrots
3 tablespoons vegetable oil
1 can (1 pound) sauerkraut, drained
1 can (1 pound) tomatoes, undrained
1 small bay leaf
1/4 teaspoon dried thyme or basil
salt, pepper to taste
1 pound fresh or frozen flounder fillets, cut up
1/8 teaspoon dill seed
1 cup sour cream at room temperature
2 tablespoons minced fresh parsley

Sauté the onion and carrots in the oil in a large skillet or Dutch oven until tender. Add the sauerkraut, and sauté, mixing with a fork, for 2-3 minutes. Add the tomatoes, bay leaf, thyme, salt and pepper and cook slowly, covered, for 20 minutes. Add the flounder and dill seed and water to cover. Cover and cook slowly until the fish is just tender, about 10 minutes. Mix in the sour cream and leave on the stove long enough to heat through. Serve garnished with the parsley. Serves 4.

MENU

Flounder-Sauerkraut Smetana Stew
Warm Parkerhouse Rolls
Cherry Pie à la mode

Spanish Beef-Eggplant Stew

An excellent autumn supper dish.

1 large onion, peeled and chopped
1-2 garlic cloves, crushed
1/4 cup olive or vegetable oil
3 medium-sized tomatoes, peeled and chopped
1 teaspoon paprika
1/2 teaspoon dried oregano
salt, pepper to taste
2 pounds chuck or stew beef, cut into 1½-inch cubes
1 cup (about) beef bouillon or water
1 medium-sized eggplant, washed, stemmed and cut
into small cubes
1/3 cup chopped fresh parsley

In a kettle sauté the onion and garlic in the oil until tender. Mix in the tomatoes, paprika, oregano, salt and pepper. Cook slowly, uncovered, for 5 minutes. Push aside and add the beef cubes, several at a time, and brown in the oil drippings. Add the bouillon or water and bring to a boil. Lower the heat and cook slowly, covered, for 1 hour. Add the eggplant cubes and continue to cook slowly for about 30 minutes longer, or until the ingredients are tender. Mix in the parsley just before serving. Serves 4 to 6.

MENU

Spanish Beef-Eggplant Stew
Crusty White Bread
Fresh Orange Slices with Grated Coconut

Pork and Rice Stew, Chinese-Style

1 cup minced green onions, with tops
2 garlic cloves, crushed
6 tablespoons (about) peanut oil
4 pounds lean boneless pork, cut into 1-inch cubes
2½ cups uncooked long grain rice
5 cups (about) beef bouillon or water
1/3 cup (about) soy sauce
4 slices fresh ginger (optional)
2 teaspoons sugar
pepper to taste
1 can (1 pound) bean sprouts, drained
1 can (8 ounces) bamboo shoots, sliced and drained
1 can (8 ounces) water chestnuts, drained and sliced
3 cups sliced fresh or canned mushrooms
2 medium-sized green peppers, cleaned and sliced

Sauté the onions and garlic in the oil in a kettle until tender. Dry the pork cubes. Push aside the onions and add the pork cubes, several at a time, to brown on all sides. Add more oil, if needed. Add a little water and cook slowly, covered, for 30 minutes. Add the rice, bouillon, soy sauce, ginger, sugar and pepper and mix well. Cover and cook slowly for about 30 minutes or until the ingredients are tender and the liquid is absorbed. Mix in the remaining ingredients and cook another 10 minutes. (The cook may wish to add more soy sauce when adding the last six ingredients. The strength of soy sauce varies considerably, so it is difficult to stipulate the necessary amount for any recipe.) Serves 10 to 12.

MENU

Pork and Rice Stew, Chinese-Style
Assorted Crackers
Fresh Fruit Medley
Almond Cookies

Mulligan Stew

This stew, originally prepared by hobos, was made of any available meats and vegetables, and for some unknown reason came to be known by the Irish name of Mulligan. Over the years the so-called recipes for it have included any number of diverse ingredients, and seemingly every cook has a different version. This is one of the many.

2½ pounds beef chuck or stew beef, cut into 1½-inch cubes
4 tablespoons flour
salt, pepper to taste
3-4 tablespoons shortening
8 cups water
4 large carrots, scraped and sliced thickly
6 medium-sized potatoes, peeled and halved
1 medium-sized head cauliflower, cleaned and cut up
4 large onions, peeled and halved
2 cups green peas
2 cups whole kernel corn
1/2 teaspoon dried thyme
1/2 teaspoon dried marjoram
1/4 cup chopped fresh parsley

Dry the beef cubes and dredge with flour seasoned with salt and pepper. Heat the shortening in a kettle or Dutch oven and brown the meat in it on all sides. Add the water and bring to a boil. Lower the heat, cover and simmer for 1½ hours or until the meat is almost tender. Add the carrots, potatoes, cauliflower and onions and cook 30 minutes. Then add the remaining ingredients and cook about 12 minutes, or until the vegetables are cooked. Serves 8.

MENU

Mulligan Stew
Crusty White Bread
Butterscotch Sundaes

Sweet-Sour Pork-Red Cabbage Stew

A good winter dish, typical of the cooking of Germany and Austria.

1 large onion, peeled and chopped
3 tablespoons lard or shortening
2 pounds lean boneless pork, cut into 1½-inch cubes
1 bay leaf
3 whole cloves
salt, pepper to taste
1 medium-sized head red cabbage, cleaned and
finely shredded
2 tart apples, peeled and cubed
1/2 cup wine vinegar
3 tablespoons sugar
3 tablespoons currant jelly (optional)

Fry the onion in the lard in a skillet or Dutch oven until tender. Add the pork and brown on all sides. Add the bay leaf, cloves, salt and pepper, and water to cover. Cover and cook slowly for 1 hour. Add the cabbage and apple and more water, if needed. Continue to cook slowly for about 30 minutes longer, or until the cabbage is tender. Add the vinegar, sugar and jelly during the last 10 minutes of cooking. Serves 6.

MENU

Sweet-Sour Pork-Red Cabbage Stew
Rye Bread
Apple Kuchen

African Chicken-Peanut Butter Stew

The peanut, called a groundnut in Africa, is an essential ingredient in the basic cookery of many countries. Peanut sauces are particularly important to the many West African stews, especially those made with chicken. Generally this dish is flavored with a number of pungent seasonings in addition to the peanut sauce. The following stew is an adaptation that is prepared with peanut butter as a substitute for the homemade ground mixture.

1 frying chicken, about 3½ pounds, cut up
1 large onion, peeled and sliced
2 garlic cloves, crushed
4 tablespoons peanut or vegetable oil
3 large tomatoes, peeled and chopped
1/4 cup tomato paste
2 red or green chilies, washed and seeded, or
1 tablespoon canned chopped green chilies
salt, pepper to taste
1/2 cup (about) peanut butter

Wash the chicken pieces and dry. Sauté the onion and garlic in the oil in a large skillet until tender. Push aside and add the tomatoes, tomato paste, chilies, salt and pepper. Leave uncovered and cook slowly for 5 minutes. Add the chicken pieces and cook in some of the drippings, pushing the sauce aside, until brown. Cover with water, cover and cook slowly for 25 minutes. Mix the peanut butter with some of the hot sauce and stir well. Mix into the chicken and leave on the stove several minutes longer. Check the sauce to determine whether you would like to add more peanut butter. Serves 4.

MENU

African Chicken-Peanut Butter Stew
Warm Corn Muffins
Banana Cream Pie

Easy Veal-Vegetable Stew

A delicious easy-to-prepare stew for a family meal.

1½ pounds stewing veal, cut into 1½-inch cubes
2 tablespoons flour
salt, pepper to taste
1/4 cup vegetable oil or shortening
1 can (1 pound) tomatoes, undrained
1/4 teaspoon dried marjoram or thyme
1 package (9 ounces) frozen cut green beans
1 package (10 ounces) frozen cut corn
1 can (1 pound) small white onions, drained
3 tablespoons chopped fresh parsley

Dry the veal cubes and dust with flour seasoned with salt and pepper. Heat the oil in a skillet or large saucepan and brown the veal in it on all sides. Add the tomatoes, marjoram and water to cover. Cover and simmer for 1½ hours, adding more water during the cooking, if needed. Add the vegetables during the last 10 or 15 minutes of cooking. Mix in the parsley before removing from the stove. Serves 4.

MENU

Easy Veal-Vegetable Stew
Warm Whole-Wheat Rolls
Ice Cream Cake

Short Ribs Jardinière

This is an inviting way to prepare inexpensive short ribs.

4-4½ pounds beef short ribs, cut into 3-inch pieces
flour
salt, pepper to taste
1/4 cup (about) shortening or vegetable oil
2 large onions, peeled and sliced
2 garlic cloves, crushed
1 can (6 ounces) tomato paste
2 cups hot water
2 bay leaves

1/4 teaspoon dried rosemary
2 carrots, scraped and sliced
1 package (9 ounces) frozen cut green beans

Dry the short ribs and dredge with flour that has been seasoned with salt and pepper. Set aside on a plate. Heat the shortening in a skillet and sauté the onions and garlic in it until tender. Push aside and add the short ribs to brown on all sides. Mix in the tomato paste and add the hot water. Mix well. Add the bay leaves and rosemary. Cover and cook slowly for 1½ hours. Add the carrots and cook another 30 minutes, adding the green beans during the last 10 minutes of cooking. Serves 4.

MENU

Short Ribs Jardinière
Crusty White Bread
Lemon Chiffon Cake

Southern Chicken with Dumplings

A simple but good dish for an impromptu meal.

2 pounds chicken thighs
2 cups water
1/2 teaspoon dried parsley
salt, pepper to taste
2 cups frozen mixed vegetables
1 can (1 pound) small white onions, drained
1 cup packaged biscuit mix
1/3 cup milk

Put the chicken, water, parsley, salt and pepper in a large saucepan or kettle. Cover and simmer for 40 minutes or until the chicken is tender. Mix in the vegetables and onions. Combine the biscuit mix and milk and stir lightly. Drop by spoonfuls over the chicken pieces. Cook, uncovered, 10 minutes. Cover and cook 10 minutes longer or until the biscuits are done. Serves 4.

MENU

Southern Chicken with Dumplings
Mixed Green Salad
Chilled Watermelon

Weekend Meatball-Rice Stew

Excellent to serve at a Saturday or Sunday night supper.

1½ pounds ground beef
1 egg, slightly beaten
1 cup fine cracker crumbs
1/4 cup minced onion
2 teaspoons turmeric powder (optional)
salt, pepper to taste
3 tablespoons (about) vegetable oil or shortening
1 can (10½ ounces) condensed tomato soup
1 soup can water
1/4 teaspoon dried thyme or oregano
2 cups frozen baby lima beans
2 cups cooked rice

In a bowl combine the beef, egg, crumbs, onion, turmeric, salt and pepper. Shape into about 24 meatballs. Brown a few at a time in the oil in a large saucepan, or Dutch oven. Mix in the soup, water and thyme. Season with salt and pepper. Cover and cook slowly for 20 minutes. Check now and then to see if a little water is needed to prevent the meatballs from sticking to the pan. Stir in the lima beans and rice and cook about 7 minutes longer, or until the ingredients are cooked. Serves 6.

MENU

Weekend Meatball-Rice Stew
Hot Buttered French Bread
Strawberry Chiffon Pie

Leftover Ham-Lentil Pot

This dish is good and economical.

1 cup dried lentils
1 large onion, peeled and minced
2 garlic cloves, crushed
2 tablespoons vegetable oil
1 can (6 ounces) tomato paste
salt, pepper to taste
1 teaspoon prepared mustard
1 teaspoon Worcestershire sauce
3 cups cubed cooked ham

Wash and pick over the lentils. In a large saucepan or
Dutch oven sauté the onion and garlic in the oil until tender. Add the lentils and 3 cups water. Bring to a boil; boil
for 2 minutes. Take off the heat and let stand for 1 hour.
Return to the stove and mix in the tomato paste, salt and
pepper. Cover and cook slowly for 1 hour or until the lentils
are tender. Mix in the mustard, Worcestershire and ham and
leave on the stove for 5 minutes. Serves 4 to 6.

MENU

Leftover Ham-Lentil Pot
Crusty Dark Bread
Chocolate Nut Cake

Lamb Curry with Peas

This is a type of stew that originated in India many, many years ago. Curry, an important seasoning in Indian cuisine, varies in strength depending on its brand, so you may want to experiment to find the brand and amount that suits your taste.

1 large onion, peeled and minced
2 tablespoons vegetable oil
1-3 tablespoons curry powder
salt, pepper to taste
1/3 cup flour
1 cup chicken broth
2 cups milk
3 cups diced cooked lamb
2 cups green peas

Sauté the onion in the oil in a large saucepan until tender. Add the curry powder, salt and pepper and cook 1 minute. Stir in the flour and then gradually add the broth, stirring as adding, and cook slowly until thickened. Pour in the milk and cook slowly until thickened and smooth. Mix in the lamb and cook slowly for 10 minutes. Then add the peas and cook for 5 minutes. Serves 4.

MENU

Lamb Curry with Peas
Hot Baking Powder Biscuits
Gingered Pineapple Slices

Pork Goulash with Noodles

A different type of goulash, this dish is good for a winter supper or dinner.

2 pounds lean boneless pork, cut into 1½-inch cubes
2 large onions, peeled and sliced
1/4 cup lard or shortening
1-2 tablespoons paprika
1 can (6 ounces) tomato paste
1/2 teaspoon caraway seeds
1 bay leaf
salt, pepper to taste
1 large green pepper, cleaned and chopped
3 cups drained cooked noodles

Dry the pork cubes. Sauté the onions in the lard in a large skillet until tender. Add the paprika and cook 1 minute. Push aside and add the pork cubes, several at a time, and brown in the drippings. Mix in the tomato paste, caraway seeds, bay leaf and water to cover. Season with salt and pepper. Cook slowly, covered, for 1½ hours, adding more water if necessary. Stir in the green pepper and noodles. Leave on the stove long enough to heat through. Remove and discard the bay leaf. Serves 6.

MENU

Pork Goulash with Noodles
Salt Sticks
Fruit-Filled Pancakes

Oxtail Stew Paysanne

Oxtails, a flavorful meat, are often difficult to find, but are well worth looking for as they make interesting dishes such as this one.

2 pounds oxtails, cut into short lengths
flour
salt, pepper to taste
1 large onion, peeled and chopped
1-2 garlic cloves, crushed

1/4 cup diced bacon
2 tablespoons vegetable oil
2 cups (about) beef bouillon or water
1 bay leaf
1/4 teaspoon dried thyme
2 large carrots, scraped and sliced thickly
4 medium-sized potatoes, peeled and halved
4 small turnips, pared and cubed

Dry the oxtail pieces and dredge in flour seasoned with salt and pepper. Set aside on a plate. In a skillet sauté the onion and garlic with the bacon in the oil until tender. Push aside and add the oxtails. Brown on all sides. Add the bouillon, bay leaf and thyme. Bring to a boil. Lower the heat, cover and cook slowly for 3 hours or until tender. Add the carrots, potatoes and turnips during the last 30 minutes of cooking. Serve the oxtails surrounded by the vegetables. Serves 4.

MENU

Oxtail Stew Paysanne
Crusty Dark Bread
Cherry Torte

Pork Hock-Vegetable Stew

Inexpensive pork hocks make an interesting and different stew.

1 large onion, peeled and chopped
3 tablespoons lard or vegetable oil
4 fresh pork hocks
1 bay leaf
1/2 teaspoon celery seed
salt, pepper to taste
4 medium-sized sweet potatoes, peeled
4 medium-sized white turnips, peeled
2 cups frozen cut-up corn

In a kettle sauté the onion in the lard until tender. Push aside and add the hocks. Brown on all sides. Add the bay leaf, celery seed, salt and pepper and water to cover. Bring to a boil. Lower the heat, cover and simmer for 1½ hours. Add the sweet potatoes and turnips and a little more water, if needed. Continue cooking for another 30 minutes or until the ingredients are done. Add the corn during the last 5 minutes of cooking. Serve the hocks on a platter surrounded with the vegetables. Serves 4.

MENU

Pork Hock-Vegetable Stew
Warm Corn Muffins
Pecan Pie

RAGOUTS

Taken from the French word *ragoûter*, meaning "to revive the taste," a ragout denotes a stew that is generally highly seasoned, perhaps with wine, spices or other flavorings.

Prepared with meat, game, poultry or fish, and sometimes with vegetables, ragouts rarely require elaborate ingredients. Some of the best-known brown ragouts are those with mutton or lamb. On the other hand, excellent white ragouts feature such foods as lobster, asparagus tips and truffles. A particular favorite is *civet*, generally made with small game such as hare or rabbit.

Although primarily thought of as a French dish, other cuisines have versions of ragouts. A good ragout can be made with whatever the cook wishes.

Marvelous for sit-down dinners, holidays, or small late-evening get-togethers, a ragout deserves to be served regally with pretty table appointments.

Ragout of Sirloin Tips Jardinière

This elegant ragout is a good dish for a holiday dinner.

3 tablespoons flour
salt and pepper to taste
3 pounds sirloin beef tips, cut into 1½-inch cubes
2 medium-sized onions, peeled and sliced thinly
3-4 tablespoons butter, margarine or vegetable oil
1½ cups (about) dry red wine
1 teaspoon crumbled dried herbs (chives, basil,
thyme or oregano)
1 package (9 ounces) frozen artichoke hearts or
1/2 pound small, fresh artichoke hearts, if available
1 package (10 ounces) frozen cauliflower or
1/2 head fresh cauliflower, broken into small pieces
1 package (10 ounces) frozen zucchini or
1/2 pound fresh zucchini, unpeeled and chopped
2 tablespoons chopped fresh parsley

Put the flour, salt and pepper in a plastic or paper bag and shake the beef cubes in it. Sauté the onions in the heated butter or other fat in a large skillet or saucepan. Push aside and add the floured beef cubes, several at a time, and brown on all sides. Add the wine and herbs; season with salt and pepper. Cover and cook slowly for 30 minutes. Add the frozen vegetables and cook slowly another 15 minutes or longer, until the ingredients are tender. Add more wine during the cooking, if needed. Stir in the parsley. Serves 6 to 8. *Note: If using fresh vegetables, add the cauliflower 30 minutes before the ragout is done; add the remaining vegetables 15 minutes before the end of cooking.*

MENU

Ragout of Sirloin Tips Jardinière
Buttered Boiled Potatoes or Noodles
Warm Croissants
French Pastry

Veal Ragout à la Niçoise

This ragout is prepared in the style of Nice, a resort city in southern France. It includes traditional Niçoise ingredients such as garlic, tomatoes and olives. It is a delectable dish for a sit-down company dinner.

3 pounds boneless shoulder of veal, cut into 1½-inch cubes
3-4 tablespoons olive or vegetable oil
salt, pepper to taste
2 large onions, peeled and sliced
2-3 garlic cloves, crushed
1 cup tomato purée
1½ cups (about) dry white wine
1/4 teaspoon crumbled dried thyme
1/4 teaspoon crumbled dried tarragon
12 flat anchovies, drained and minced
1 cup pitted black olives
3 tablespoons chopped fresh parsley

Dry the veal cubes and brown several at a time in the heated oil in a large skillet. Season with salt and pepper. Remove or push aside and add the onions and garlic. Sauté until tender. Mix the veal cubes with the onions and garlic. Mix in the tomato purée. Add the wine, thyme and tarragon. Bring to a boil. Reduce the heat, cover and cook slowly for about 1½ hours or until the meat is tender. Add more wine during the cooking if needed. Stir in the anchovies, olives and parsley and cook another 5 minutes. Serves 6.

MENU

Veal Ragout à la Niçoise
Buttered Rice
Romaine Lettuce Salad
French Bread
Fresh Strawberry Tarts

Ragout Of Lamb Bonne Femme

Traditional names of foods sometimes have unusual meanings. *Bonne femme*, for example, means "a good wife" in French. In cookery, however, it refers to a preparation of ingredients with mushrooms and white wine. This ragout, which also includes potatoes and tomatoes, is a good spring or summer dinner dish.

2 pounds lamb shoulder, cut into 1½-inch cubes
3-4 tablespoons vegetable oil
1 large onion, peeled and quartered
1 teaspoon sugar
3 tablespoons flour
salt, pepper to taste
1 garlic clove, crushed
1¼ cups (about) dry white wine
1/4 cup tomato purée
2 medium-sized tomatoes, peeled and chopped
***bouquet garni* (1 bay leaf, 1/2 teaspoon dried thyme,**
2 parsley sprigs)
6 medium-sized potatoes, peeled and halved
18 medium-sized whole mushrooms, cleaned
3 tablespoons butter or margarine
juice of 1 large lemon

Trim any excess fat from the lamb. Dry and brown several cubes at a time in the heated oil in a large saucepan or Dutch oven. Push aside and add the onion. Sauté until tender. Add the sugar and then the flour; mix well. Season with salt and pepper. Stir in the garlic, wine, tomato purée, tomatoes and *bouquet garni*. Bring to a boil. Lower the heat, cover and cook slowly for 1 hour. Add more wine during the cooking, if needed. Add the potatoes and continue to cook slowly for about 40 minutes longer, until the ingredients are tender. While the lamb mixture is cooking, sauté the mushrooms in the butter and lemon juice in a skillet for 3 minutes. Mix into the ragout 5 minutes before the cooking is finished. Remove and discard the bay leaf and parsley sprigs. Serves 6.

MENU

Ragout Of Lamb Bonne Femme
Mixed Green Salad
Warm Garlic Bread
Ice Cream Bombe

Continental Shrimp-and-Mushroom Ragout

Sour cream imparts a pleasing flavor to this medley of rich ingredients. A good dish for a weekend luncheon.

3 tablespoons minced green onions, with tops
3 tablespoons minced green pepper
3 tablespoons butter, margarine or vegetable oil
2 tablespoons fresh lemon juice
1/2 pound fresh mushrooms, cleaned and sliced
3 tablespoons flour
2 cups light cream or milk
1 pound cooked cleaned shrimp
1½ cups frozen green peas
1/4 teaspoon crumbled dried rosemary
salt, pepper to taste
1 cup sour cream at room temperature
1 tablespoon chopped fresh dill or parsley

Sauté the onions and peppers in the butter in a large saucepan or Dutch oven until tender. Add the lemon juice and mushrooms and sauté 4 minutes. Stir in the flour. Gradually add the cream or milk and cook slowly, stirring, until slightly thickened. Mix in the shrimp, peas and rosemary. Season with salt and pepper. Cover and cook slowly for 10 minutes or until the shrimp and peas are tender. Mix in the sour cream and dill and heat through. Serves 4.

MENU

Continental Shrimp-and-Mushroom Ragout
Buttered Rice

Escarole-Radish Salad
Warm Cloverleaf Rolls
Orange Chiffon Pie

Ragout de Boeuf Bourgeoise

Superb hearty dishes prepared *à la bourgeoise* generally include carrots and small onions as well as pieces of braised meat. They are particularly good cold-weather fare.

> **3 tablespoons flour**
> **salt, pepper to taste**
> **2½ pounds boneless beef chuck or round, cut into**
> **1½-inch cubes**
> **4 thin slices bacon, chopped**
> **2 tablespoons vegetable oil**
> **1½ cups dry vermouth or white wine**
> **3 tablespoons brandy**
> **1/2 cup beef bouillon**
> **1/8 teaspoon dried thyme**
> **1/8 teaspoon dried marjoram**
> **1 garlic clove, crushed**
> **1 small strip orange peel**
> **4 carrots, scraped and sliced thinly**
> **14 small white onions, peeled**
> **2 cups frozen cut-up green beans**

Put the flour, salt and pepper in a paper or plastic bag. Wipe the beef cubes to dry them and shake in the flour. Cook the bacon in a large skillet and add the oil. Add the beef cubes, a few at a time, and brown on all sides. Add the vermouth or wine, brandy, bouillon, thyme, marjoram, garlic and orange peel. Season with salt and pepper. Cover and cook slowly for 1 hour. Add the carrots and onions and continue to cook slowly for about 45 minutes longer, or until the ingredients are tender. Add the green beans about 12 minutes before the cooking is finished. Serves 8.

MENU

Ragout de Boeuf Bourgeoise
Sliced Tomato-Cucumber Salad
Crusty Dark Bread
Cherry Soufflé

Rabbit Ragout Chasseur

There are many superb dishes that can be prepared with the tender, mild-flavored meat of the rabbit. This one, enriched with shallots, tomatoes, white wine and mushrooms, is a good summer supper dish.

2 fryer rabbits, about 3 pounds each, cut up
1/3 cup (about) olive or vegetable oil
3 large fresh tomatoes, peeled and chopped, or
3 canned whole tomatoes, chopped
1½ cups (about) dry white wine
1 bay leaf, crumbled
1/2 teaspoon crumbled dried marjoram
salt, pepper to taste
1/4 cup chopped shallots or green onions
3 tablespoons butter or margarine
1 pound small whole or quartered large mushrooms,
cleaned
2 tablespoons minced fresh tarragon, basil or parsley

Dry the rabbit pieces. Heat the oil in a large saucepan or Dutch oven and brown the rabbit pieces, a few at a time in it until golden on all sides. Add the tomatoes, wine, bay leaf, marjoram, salt and pepper. Mix well. Cover and cook slowly 1 hour or longer or until the rabbit is tender. Add more wine during the cooking, if needed. While the rabbit is cooking, sauté the shallots or green onions in the butter in a skillet. Add the mushrooms and sauté for 3 minutes. Mix the onions, mushrooms and the tarragon into the ragout 5 minutes before the cooking is finished. Serves 6.

MENU

Rabbit Ragout Chasseur
Buttered Brown Rice
Bibb Lettuce Salad
Warm Garlic Bread
Ice Cream-Filled Cream Puffs

Balkan Veal and Pork Ragout

This is a typical ragout of the Balkan countries where flavorful meat and vegetable dishes are served at convivial family and holiday celebrations.

1½ pounds boneless veal shoulder,
cut into 1½-inch cubes
1½ pounds lean boneless pork,
cut into 1½-inch cubes
flour
salt, pepper to taste
3 tablespoons (about) vegetable oil
2 garlic cloves, crushed
2 large onions, peeled and sliced
1 cup (about) hot bouillon or water
1/2 cup dry white wine
1/2 teaspoon crumbled dried thyme or oregano
3 large carrots, scraped and cut into 1½-inch pieces
8 small or 4 medium potatoes, peeled and cut into halves
1 package (10 ounces) frozen zucchini or
1/2 pound fresh zucchini
1 tablespoon chopped fresh dill or parsley

Dry the meat cubes and sprinkle with flour, salt and pepper. In a large pan brown a few meat cubes at a time in the oil. Push aside and add the garlic and onions. Sauté until tender. Add the bouillon, wine, thyme, salt and pepper. Bring to a boil. Lower the heat, cover and cook slowly for 1½ hours. Add the carrots after cooking 1 hour. After cooking 1½ hours, add the potatoes and continue cooking another 30 minutes longer, or until the ingredients are tender. Mix in the zucchini 20 minutes before the end of the cooking. Stir in the dill when the ragout is finished cooking. Serves 8.

MENU

Balkan Veal and Pork Ragout
Romaine Lettuce Salad
Crusty Dark Bread
Honey or Spice Cake

Ragout de Veau Marengo

An excellent veal ragout that could be served for a late evening supper.

3 pounds shoulder veal, cut into 1½-inch cubes
3-4 tablespoons olive or vegetable oil
1 large onion, peeled and chopped
2 tablespoons flour
1 cup dry white wine
3/4 cup beef bouillon
1/2 cup tomato purée
2 garlic cloves, halved
bouquet garni (1 bay leaf, 1/2 teaspoon dried thyme,
2 parsley sprigs)
1 small strip orange peel
salt, pepper to taste
1/2 pound fresh mushrooms, cleaned
3 tablespoons chopped fresh parsley

Dry the veal cubes and brown, a few pieces at a time, in the heated oil in a skillet. Push aside and add the onion. Sauté until tender. Stir in the flour. Pour in the wine and bouillon and bring to a boil. Boil for 1 minute. Stir in the tomato purée, garlic, *bouquet garni*, orange peel, salt and pepper. Lower the heat, cover and cook slowly for 1¼ hours or until the meat is tender. Add the mushrooms during the last 10 minutes of cooking. Stir in the parsley just before serving. Remove and discard the bay leaf and parsley sprigs. Serves 6.

MENU

Ragout de Veau Marengo
Parsley Boiled Potatoes
Hearts of Lettuce Salad
Warm Garlic Bread
Peach Short Cake

Ragout of Chicken Orientale

This is an especially good summer luncheon dish.

8 large chicken breasts, split in half
6 tablespoons (about) peanut or vegetable oil
salt, pepper to taste
2/3 cup pineapple juice
4-6 tablespoons soy sauce
1 cup chicken broth or bouillon
1 cup wine vinegar
2/3 cup sliced water chestnuts
2/3 cup sugar
6 tablespoons minced fresh ginger
3 cups drained crushed pineapple
6 tablespoons cornstarch
1/2 cup water
2 large green peppers, cleaned and chopped

Remove the skin from each chicken breast. Sauté the chicken breasts on both sides in the oil in a large kettle or skillet. Season with salt and pepper. Add the pineapple juice, cover and cook slowly for 15 minutes. Remove from the stove and cool. With a knife take off all the meat from the breasts. Discard the bones. Cut the meat into bite-sized pieces and return to the cooking dish. Add the soy sauce, chicken broth, vinegar, water chestnuts, sugar, ginger and pineapple. Cook slowly, covered, for 30 minutes, long enough to blend the flavors. Dissolve the cornstarch in the water and stir into the chicken mixture. Cook slowly, stirring frequently, for several minutes, until thickened. Add the green peppers just before removing from the heat. Serves 8.

MENU

Ragout of Chicken Orientale
Buttered Rice or Fine Noodles
Snow Peas Vinaigrette
Crisp Crackers
Fresh Fruit
Almond Cookies

Basque Ragout of Lamb and Vegetables

The Basque region of northwest Spain and southwest France is famous for its good cooking. Fine ingredients typical of the area are used in this appealing ragout. A good dish for a Sunday supper.

2 pounds lamb shoulder, cut into 1½-inch cubes
3 tablespoons olive or vegetable oil
1 large onion, peeled and sliced
1 garlic clove, crushed
1 medium-sized eggplant, about 1¼ pounds,
unpeeled and cut into small cubes
1 can (6 ounces) tomato paste
1½ cups (about) hot water
1/4 teaspoon each of crumbled dried thyme and marjoram
salt, pepper to taste
6 medium-sized potatoes, peeled and halved
1 jar (4 ounces) pimientos, chopped
2 tablespoons chopped fresh parsley

Remove any excess fat from the lamb. Dry and brown a few pieces at a time in the oil in a kettle. Push aside and add the onion and garlic. Sauté until tender. Add the eggplant, tomato paste, water, thyme, marjoram, salt and pepper and mix well. Cover and cook slowly 1 hour. Add the potatoes and cook about 30 minutes longer or until tender. Pour in a little more water during the cooking, if needed. Add the pimientos and parsley 5 minutes before the cooking is finished. Serves 6.

MENU

Basque Ragout of Lamb and Vegetables
Mixed Green Salad
Warm Garlic Bread
Orange Bavarian Cream

Ragout de Boeuf Bordelaise

This flavorful stew, made with a good dry red wine from the region of Bordeaux, is one of the best French ragouts.

3 pounds beef sirloin, round or chuck,
cut into 2-inch cubes
flour
salt, pepper to taste
1/4 cup olive or vegetable oil
3/4 cup minced green onions, with tops
1 large garlic clove, crushed
2 cups (about) red Bordeaux wine
2 parsley sprigs
1 small bay leaf
1/2 teaspoon dried thyme
1/2 pound fresh mushrooms, cleaned and sliced
lengthwise into halves
1 can (1 pound) small white onions, drained

Dry the beef cubes and dredge with flour, seasoned with salt and pepper. Brown on all sides in the heated oil in a large kettle. Push aside and add the green onions and garlic. Sauté until tender. Add the wine, parsley, bay leaf and thyme. Season with salt and pepper. Bring to a boil. Lower the heat, cover and cook slowly about 1½ hours or until the meat is tender. Add the mushrooms and onions 10 minutes before the cooking is finished. Remove and discard the parsley sprigs and bay leaf. Serves 6.

MENU

Ragout de Boeuf Bordelaise
Buttered Green Noodles
Endive Salad
French Bread
Babas au Rhum

Duckling Civet

Although the French word *civet* is used generally for ragouts made with small game and flavored with red wine, mushrooms and onions, the word is derived from *cive*, which means green onions. Probably they were an important ingredient when the dish was created. Duckling is a good substitute for the game. This is an elegant company dinner.

4 thin slices bacon, chopped
2-3 tablespoons vegetable oil
6 shallots or green onions, with tops, minced
1-2 garlic cloves, crushed
2 ducklings, 4-5 pounds each, cut into serving pieces
3 tablespoons flour
1½ cups (about) dry red wine
1 cup beef bouillon
1/4 cup tomato purée
1/3 cup brandy
1 bay leaf
3 parsley sprigs
1/4 teaspoon dried thyme
1/4 teaspoon dried rosemary

salt, pepper to taste
24 small white onions, peeled
24 whole mushrooms, cleaned

Cook the bacon in a large kettle for 1 or 2 minutes. Add the oil, shallots or onions, and garlic; sauté until tender. Add the duckling pieces, a few at a time, and brown on all sides. Mix in the flour to blend well. Add the wine, bouillon, purée, brandy, bay leaf, parsley, thyme, rosemary, salt and pepper. Mix and bring to a boil. Lower the heat, cover and cook slowly for 1 hour. Add the onions and continue to cook slowly about 30 minutes longer, or until the ducklings and onions are tender. Add the mushrooms during the last 10 minutes of cooking. Remove and discard the bay leaf and parsley. Serves 6 to 8.

MENU

Duckling Civet
Parsley Potatoes
Bibb Lettuce Salad
French Bread
Camembert Cheese

Curried Lamb Ragout Indienne

Yogurt is a main ingredient of this ragout.

1 large onion, peeled and chopped
1 garlic clove, crushed
1/4 cup peanut or vegetable oil
1 teaspoon ground turmeric
1 teaspoon ground coriander (optional)
1-2 tablespoons curry powder
salt, pepper to taste
2 pounds boneless lamb, trimmed of fat,
cut into 1½-inch cubes

1/2 cup (about) tomato juice
1 cup plain yogurt at room temperature

Sauté the onion and garlic in the oil in a large saucepan or Dutch oven. Stir in the turmeric, coriander, curry powder, salt and pepper. Cook 1 minute. Dry the lamb cubes and brown, several at a time, on all sides. Add the tomato juice and bring to a boil. Lower the heat and cook slowly, covered, for 1 hour. Stir in the yogurt and continue to cook slowly for another 30 minutes, or until the ingredients are cooked. Add more tomato juice during the first hour of cooking, if needed. Serves 6.

MENU

Curried Lamb Ragout Indienne
Boiled Rice
Mixed Green Salad
Crisp Crackers
Lemon Sherbet with Chocolate Sauce

Chinese Pork-Vegetable Ragout

A flavorful Oriental ragout that is good for a Sunday night supper.

6 green onions, with tops, chopped
2 garlic cloves, crushed
3 thin slices gingerroot (optional)
1/4 cup peanut or vegetable oil
2 pounds lean boneless pork, cut into 1½-inch cubes
1 cup soy sauce
2 tablespoons dry sherry
2 tablespoons sugar
pepper to taste
2 cups shredded Chinese cabbage
2 cups shredded spinach

1 cup sliced mushrooms
1 package (6 ounces) snow peas
1/2 cup sliced bamboo shoots

Sauté the onions, garlic and gingerroot in the oil in a large wok or skillet until tender. Add the pork, several cubes at a time, and brown on all sides. Add the soy sauce, sherry, sugar and pepper. Cover and cook slowly for 1 hour. Add a little water during the cooking, if needed. Mix in the cabbage, spinach, mushrooms, snow peas and bamboo shoots. Continue cooking for about 15 minutes, or until the ingredients are tender. The vegetables should not cook too long. Serves 6.

MENU

Chinese Pork-Vegetable Ragout
Steamed Rice
Orange Sherbet with Chopped Pineapple

Lamb-Eggplant Ragout Italiana

This ragout, made with favorite Italian foods, is good for a weekend luncheon.

3 pounds boneless shoulder or leg of lamb, cut into
1½-inch cubes
3 medium-sized onions, peeled and chopped
2 garlic cloves, crushed
6 tablespoons (about) olive or vegetable oil
1 can (6 ounces) tomato paste
2 cups (about) dry red wine
1 bay leaf
1/2 teaspoon dried thyme
salt, pepper to taste
1 large eggplant, stemmed and cubed
3 tablespoons chopped fresh parsley

Dry the lamb cubes and set aside. In a large saucepan sauté the onions and garlic in the oil until tender. Push aside and add the lamb, several cubes at a time, and brown on all sides. Mix in the tomato paste. Add the wine, bay leaf, thyme, salt and pepper. Cook slowly, covered, for 1 hour, adding more wine, if needed. Add the eggplant and continue cooking for about 30 minutes longer, or until the ingredients are cooked. Remove and discard the bay leaf. Mix in the parsley. Serves 6 to 8.

MENU

Lamb-Eggplant Ragout Italiana
Warm Garlic Bread
Canned Pears with Whipped Cream

Viennese Oxtail Ragout

This is another excellent oxtail dish, good for a winter dinner.

2 pounds oxtails, cut into short lengths
flour
salt, pepper to taste
2 medium-sized onions, peeled and chopped
2 carrots, scraped and diced
1/4 cup shortening
2 tablespoons paprika
2 cups (about) beef bouillon
1/4 teaspoon dried oregano
2 cups frozen green peas
1 cup sour cream at room temperature
1 tablespoon chopped fresh dill or parsley

Dry the oxtail pieces and dredge in flour seasoned with salt and pepper. Set aside on a plate. In a saucepan sauté the onions and carrots in the shortening until tender. Mix in the paprika and cook for 1 minute. Push aside and add the oxtails. Brown on all sides. Add the bouillon and oregano and bring to a boil. Lower the heat, cover and cook slowly for 2½-3 hours until tender. Add more bouillon during the cooking, if needed. Mix in the peas, sour cream and dill and heat through. Serves 4.

MENU

Viennese Oxtail Ragout
Warm Boiled Potatoes
Poppy-Seed Rolls
Chocolate Torte

Shrimp and Artichoke Ragout

An elegant ragout that would be good for a light luncheon.

1/2 cup minced green onions, with tops
1/3 cup minced green pepper
1/4 cup minced celery
3 tablespoons butter or margarine
1 can (1 pound) tomatoes, undrained
1 can (8 ounces) tomato sauce
1 cup (about) dry white wine
1 medium bay leaf
1/2 teaspoon dried thyme
2 parsley sprigs
dash cayenne
salt, pepper to taste
1½ pounds raw shrimp, shelled and deveined
2 packages (9 ounces each) frozen artichoke hearts

In a saucepan or skillet sauté the onions, green pepper and celery in the butter until tender. Mix in the tomatoes, tomato sauce, wine, bay leaf, thyme, parsley, cayenne, salt and pepper. Cook slowly, uncovered, for 10 minutes. Add the shrimp, cover and continue cooking for 30 minutes. Add the artichoke hearts and cook about 10 minutes longer or until the ingredients are tender. Remove the bay leaf and parsley before serving. Serves 6.

MENU

Shrimp and Artichoke Ragout
Buttered Cooked Rice
Warm Whole-Wheat Rolls
Lemon Meringue Pie

Boeuf en Piperade Ragout

Another ragout from southern France, this is good for an informal company buffet.

3 pounds boneless beef chuck or stew beef, cut into
2-inch cubes
flour
salt, pepper to taste
2 large onions, peeled and sliced
2 garlic cloves, crushed
5 tablespoons (about) olive or vegetable oil
3 large tomatoes, peeled and chopped
1 can (8 ounces) tomato sauce
1 teaspoon dried basil or oregano
***bouquet garni* (1 bay leaf, 1/2 teaspoon dried thyme,**
4 parsley sprigs, wrapped in cheesecloth)
1½ cups (about) dry red wine
2 medium-sized green peppers, cleaned and sliced
2 cans pimientos, cut into strips
1 cup sliced pitted green or black olives

Dry the beef cubes and dredge in flour seasoned with salt and pepper. Set aside. In a large skillet sauté the onions and garlic in the oil until tender. Push aside and add the beef cubes, several at a time, and brown on all sides. Add more oil, if needed. Add the tomatoes, tomato sauce, basil and *bouquet garni*. Pour in the wine, cover and cook slowly for 1½ hours, adding more wine, if needed. Mix in the remaining ingredients and cook another 5 minutes, until the ingredients are tender. Remove the *bouquet garni*. Serves 6 to 8.

MENU

Boeuf en Piperade Ragout
Warm Garlic Bread
Ice Cream-Filled Cream Puffs

Ragout of Pork Stroganoff

This sour cream-flavored pork dish is elegant enough for a company dinner.

2 pounds lean boneless pork
6 tablespoons (about) butter or margarine
1 medium-sized onion, peeled and chopped
1/2 pound fresh mushrooms, cleaned and sliced
3 tablespoons tomato paste
1 tablespoon prepared mustard
1 cup dry white wine
pinch sugar
salt, pepper to taste
2 teaspoons flour
1 cup sour cream at room temperature

Remove any fat from the pork and cut into strips about 1 inch thick and 3 inches long. Heat 2 tablespoons of butter in a large saucepan or skillet. Add some of the pork and brown quickly. Remove to a plate. Finish browning the pork. Sauté the onion in the drippings. Add the mushrooms and more butter, if needed. Sauté 4 minutes. Stir in the tomato paste and mustard. Add the wine, sugar, salt and pepper. Bring to a boil. Lower the heat, cover and cook slowly for 10 minutes. Combine the flour and sour cream and leave on the stove long enough to cook slightly, 5 to 7 minutes. Serves 4.

MENU

Ragout of Pork Stroganoff
Buttered Rice

Mixed Green Salad
Crusty White Bread
French Pastries

Côte d'Azur Chicken-Vegetable Ragout

This highly seasoned ragout originated on France's southern coast. It is a good dish for a late evening supper.

**1 frying chicken, about 2½ pounds, cut up
2 medium-sized onions, peeled and sliced
1-2 garlic cloves, crushed
1/4 cup butter or margarine
3 large tomatoes, peeled and chopped
1½ cups (about) dry white wine
1 teaspoon dried tarragon or basil
salt, pepper to taste
2 medium zucchini, sliced
2 medium green peppers, cleaned and sliced
3 tablespoons chopped fresh parsley**

Dry the chicken pieces and set aside. In a skillet sauté the onions and garlic in the butter until tender. Push aside and add the chicken. Brown on all sides until golden. Add the tomatoes, wine, tarragon, salt and pepper. Cover and cook slowly for 15 minutes. Add the zucchini and peppers and continue cooking about 20 minutes longer, or until the ingredients are tender. Mix in the parsley before serving. Serves 4.

MENU

Côte d'Azur Chicken-Vegetable Ragout
Crusty White Bread
Strawberry Ice Cream with Chocolate Sauce

Fruited Lamb and Rice Ragout

This is an excellent dish to serve at an outdoor meal.

**2 pounds boneless lamb shoulder or leg,
cut into 2-inch cubes
1/2 cup diced celery
1/2 cup diced onion
1/2 cup diced green pepper
1/4 cup butter or margarine
2 cups (about) orange juice
1 teaspoon grated orange rind
dash nutmeg
salt, pepper to taste
2 cups cooked rice
1 cup diced fresh oranges
1 cup diced fresh or canned peaches
1 cup diced fresh or canned pears
1 tablespoon chopped fresh mint**

Trim any excess fat from the lamb cubes. Wipe dry and set aside. Sauté the celery, onion and green pepper in the butter in a Dutch oven. When tender push aside, and add the lamb cubes, several at a time, and brown on all sides. Add the orange juice, orange rind, nutmeg, salt and pepper. Cover and cook slowly for 1½ hours, adding more juice during the cooking if needed. Mix in the remaining ingredients and more juice, if necessary, and leave on the stove long enough to heat through. Serves 6.

MENU

*Fruited Lamb and Rice Ragout
Crusty White Bread
Chocolate Ice Cream with Grated Coconut*

Parisian Ragout de Sole

An easy-to-prepare ragout that could be served for a light luncheon.

3 tablespoons minced shallots or green onions
3 tablespoons butter or margarine
2 tablespoons fresh lemon juice
1 cup sliced fresh mushrooms
3 tablespoons flour
1 cup dry white wine
2½ cups (about) light cream or milk
dash cayenne
salt, pepper to taste
2 pounds sole or flounder fillets, cut into
serving pieces
1 cup cooked asparagus tips
1 cup cooked cleaned shrimp

Sauté the shallots in the butter in a large saucepan until tender. Add the lemon juice and mushrooms and sauté until tender, about 4 minutes. Mix in the flour and cook 1 minute. Slowly add the wine and then the cream or milk; stir constantly until thickened and smooth. Season with cayenne, salt and pepper. Add the fish pieces, cover and cook slowly for about 7 minutes or until they are just tender. Add a little more cream or milk, if desired. Mix in the asparagus and shrimp, and leave on the stove long enough to heat through. Serves 4 to 6.

MENU

Parisian Ragout de Sole
Buttered Rice
Warm Whole-Wheat Rolls
Ice Ceam Cake

Hawaiian Duckling Ragout

An excellent dish for a small holiday dinner.

1 duckling, 4-5 pounds, cut into serving pieces
1 tablespoon peanut or vegetable oil
1 cup orange juice

1 cup (about) pineapple juice
1 teaspoon minced gingerroot (optional)
2 tablespoons soy sauce
pepper to taste
1 cup pineapple tidbits, drained
1 medium-sized green pepper, cleaned and diced

Wash the duckling and wipe dry. Brown on all sides in hot oil in a Dutch oven for 30 minutes. Remove and pour off all the fat except 3 tablespoons. Add the orange and pineapple juices, gingerroot, soy sauce and pepper. Bring to a boil. Lower the heat, cover and cook slowly for 1½-2 hours or until tender. Add the remaining ingredients during the last 5 minutes of cooking. Serves 4.

MENU

Hawaiian Duckling Ragout
Buttered Noodles
Avocado-Lettuce Salad
Coconut Cream Cake

Swedish Seafood Ragout

A good dish for a late evening supper.

1 large onion, peeled and chopped
1/3 cup butter or margarine
3 tablespoons flour
2 cups fish or clam broth
2 cups (about) dry white wine
3 tablespoons tomato paste
1/2 teaspoon dried marjoram
salt, pepper to taste
1 pound white-fleshed fish fillets (cod, haddock,
flounder), cut into serving pieces
2 cups flaked cooked salmon
2 cups cleaned medium shrimp

2 cups sour cream at room temperature
2 tablespoons chopped fresh dill

In a large saucepan or kettle sauté the onion in the butter until tender. Mix in the flour and cook 1 minute. Gradually add the fish or clam broth, stirring as adding, and cook slowly until thickened and smooth. Add the wine, tomato paste, marjoram, salt, pepper and fish. Cover and cook slowly for about 7 minutes, or until the fish is just tender. Add more wine during the cooking, if needed. Mix in the salmon, shrimp and sour cream, and continue to cook over low heat until the ingredients are heated. Serve garnished with the dill. Serves 4.

MENU

Swedish Seafood Ragout
Boiled Small Potatoes
Cucumber Salad
Warm Berry Pie

Tuscan Sausage-Bean Ragout

This ragout comes from the northern Italian region of Tuscany, where white beans and sausages are favorite foods. It is a hearty dish, especially welcome on a winter supper table.

1 cup dried white beans
2 medium-sized onions, peeled and chopped
2 garlic cloves, crushed
3 tablespoons bacon fat or shortening
1 can (1 pound) tomatoes, undrained
1 can (6 ounces) tomato paste
1 teaspoon dried rosemary or thyme
salt, pepper to taste
1 pound pork sausage links, fried, drained and cut up
3 tablespoons chopped fresh parsley

Wash the beans and cover with cold water. Bring to a boil and boil for 2 minutes. Let stand for 1 hour. In a kettle sauté the onions and garlic in the fat until tender. Mix in the tomatoes, tomato paste, rosemary, salt and pepper. Cook slowly, uncovered, for 5 minutes. Add the beans and water. Cover and simmer for 1-1½ hours, until the beans are tender. Add more water during the cooking, if needed. Mix in the sausages 5 minutes before the cooking is finished and leave on the stove long enough to heat through. Serve garnished with the parsley. Serves 4.

MENU

Tuscan Sausage-Bean Ragout
Mixed Green Salad
Crusty White Bread
Gorgonzola Cheese
Crackers

Sherried Oyster and Chicken Ragout

A good ragout for a luncheon or a late evening supper.

2 tablespoons minced chives
2 tablespoons minced shallots or green onions
1/2 cup minced green pepper
4 tablespoons butter or margarine
3 tablespoons flour
4 cups light cream or milk
1/4 teaspoon freshly grated nutmeg
salt, pepper to taste
2 cups diced cooked chicken
1 pint fresh oysters, drained
3 tablespoons dry sherry

In a large saucepan sauté the chives, shallots and green pepper in the butter until tender. Mix in the flour and cook slowly, stirring, for 1 minute. Gradually add the cream or milk, stirring constantly, until thickened and smooth. Season with nutmeg, salt and pepper. Add the chicken and oysters and cook gently about 5 minutes, or until the edges of the oysters curl. Remove from the heat and mix in the sherry. Serve at once. Serves 4.

MENU

Sherried Oyster and Chicken Ragout
Warm White Rolls
Bibb Lettuce Salad
Bombe au Chocolat

Southwestern Ragout de Veau

A hearty highly flavored ragout that is a good outdoor dinner dish.

2½ pounds boneless veal shoulder, cut into 2-inch cubes
flour
salt, pepper to taste
2 large onions, peeled and chopped
2 garlic cloves, crushed
5 tablespoons (about) lard or vegetable oil
1-2 tablespoons chili powder
1 teaspoon crumbled dried oregano
salt, pepper to taste
1 can (1 pound) tomatoes, undrained
1 can (8 ounces) tomato sauce
dash hot pepper sauce
2 cups frozen cut-up corn
1 can (1 pound) red kidney beans
1 can (6 ounces) green chilies, chopped

Dry the veal cubes and dredge in flour seasoned with salt and pepper. In a large saucepan, sauté the onions and garlic in the lard or oil until tender. Mix in the chili powder, oregano, salt and pepper and cook 1 minute. Push aside and add the veal cubes, several at a time, and brown on all sides, adding more oil if needed. Add the tomatoes, tomato sauce, and hot pepper sauce. Cover and cook slowly for about 1½ hours, or until the veal is tender. Add a little water during the cooking, if needed. Add the corn, beans and chilies during the last 5 minutes of cooking. Serves 6.

MENU

Southwestern Ragout de Veau
Warm Corn Muffins
Peach Pie

Ragout of Salmon and Tomatoes

This is a good luncheon ragout.

1 medium-sized onion, peeled and chopped
1 medium-sized green pepper, cleaned and minced
2 tablespoons butter or margarine
3 tablespoons flour
1 cup milk
1 can (1 pound) tomatoes, undrained
1/2 teaspoon crumbled dried oregano or thyme
salt, pepper to taste
1 can (1 pound) salmon, drained and flaked

In a large saucepan sauté the onion and green pepper in the butter until the onion is tender. Mix in the flour and cook 1 minute. Gradually add the milk and the liquid of the tomatoes, stirring constantly. Cook slowly, stirring, until thickened and smooth. Add the tomatoes and break up with a spoon or fork. Add the oregano, salt and pepper and cook slowly, being careful not to boil, for 10 minutes. Mix in the salmon and cook another 5 minutes. Serves 4 to 6.

MENU

Ragout of Salmon and Tomatoes
Buttered Rice
Whole-Wheat Muffins
Cherry Cobbler

Polynesian Meatball-Fruit Ragout

A good ragout for an outdoor meal.

1 pound ground lean beef
1/2 pound ground lean pork
1/2 cup fine dry bread crumbs
2 tablespoons minced green onions
1 garlic clove, crushed
2 teaspoons minced gingerroot (optional)
2 tablespoons soy sauce
salt, pepper to taste
2-3 tablespoons peanut or vegetable oil
1½ cups beef bouillon or 1½ beef bouillon cubes
and 1½ cups water
3 tablespoons cornstarch
1/4 cup cider vinegar
1/4 cup sugar
1 can (13¼ ounces) pineapple tidbits, undrained
2 cans (11 ounces each) mandarin oranges, drained
1 cup canned apricot halves
1 large green pepper, cleaned and cubed

Combine the beef, pork, bread crumbs, onions, garlic, gingerroot, soy sauce, salt and pepper in a large bowl. Mix thoroughly. Shape into tiny balls. The mixture should make about 8 dozen meatballs. Heat 1 tablespoon of the oil in a kettle or skillet and brown the meatballs, several at a time, adding oil as needed. Add the bouillon, cover and cook slowly for 25 minutes. Combine the cornstarch with the vinegar. Then mix in the sugar. Stir into the meatball mixture. Add the juice from the pineapple tidbits and mix well. Stir in the fruits and green pepper, and cook over low heat, stirring once or twice, until the ingredients are heated. Serves 6 to 8.

MENU

Polynesian Meatball-Fruit Ragout
Buttered Egg Noodles
Crisp Crackers
Vanilla Ice Cream with Chocolate Sauce

Lobster and Crabmeat Ragout

An elegant ragout for a late evening supper.

3 tablespoons minced shallots or green onions
1/4 cup minced green peppers
1/4 cup butter or margarine
3 tablespoons flour
1/2 teaspoon grated nutmeg
1/2 teaspoon Worcestershire
dash cayenne
salt, pepper to taste
3-4 cups milk
2 cups diced cooked lobster
2 cups cleaned flaked crabmeat
1 cup heavy cream

Sauté the shallots or onions and green peppers in the butter in a large saucepan or kettle until tender. Mix in the flour to form a *roux* and cook 1 minute. Add the nutmeg, Worcestershire, cayenne, salt and pepper. Gradually add the milk, stirring as adding, and cook slowly, stirring occasionally, until thickened and smooth. Add the lobster and crabmeat and cook long enough to heat the ingredients. Gradually add the cream and cook slowly until heated. Serves 4.
Note: Vary the amount of milk according to the desired thickness of the sauce.

MENU

Lobster and Crabmeat Ragout
Romaine Salad
Warm Cloverleaf Rolls
Jam-Filled Crêpes

GLOSSARY

beurre manié
Kneaded or manipulated butter that is made by working flour and butter into tiny balls that are added to sauces, soups and stews as thickening agents. They must be added at the end of the cooking process, and the liquid should not be permitted to boil after they have been added.

blanquette
A meat or poultry stew with a lemon-flavored cream sauce. It also contains small white onions and mushrooms.

bouillon
A clarified clear broth made by simmering meat, fish or vegetables with seasonings in liquid and then straining. The process is designed to extract their flavors. It is served alone as a soup or used as a base in making soups, stews and sauces.

bouillon cube
A concentrated, dehydrated form of bouillon that is a convenient substitute for the homemade variety.

bouquet garni   Aromatic herbs, fresh and/or dried, which are tied together or enclosed in a small cheesecloth bag and used during cooking to flavor stocks, soups and stews. It usually includes parsley, thyme and bay leaf, to which spices can be added. The *bouquet garni* is always removed and discarded before the dish is served.

braise   Long, slow process of cooking meats and vegetables that includes browning in a little fat and then simmering, tightly covered, in a small amount of liquid. Braising is generally done on top of the stove, but sometimes is done in the oven.

broth   An unclarified thin liquid in which meat, fish or vegetables have been cooked. It is also a soup.

burgoo   A thick stew made with various kinds of meats and vegetables, traditionally cooked in Kentucky in large iron pots for outdoor get-togethers.

casserole   A deep heavy dish with a tight-fitting lid in which foods can be cooked slowly. Also, a combination of foods that were cooked slowly on top of the stove or in the oven.

civet   A ragout generally made with small game, particularly rabbit, red wine, onions, mushrooms and the blood of the animal. This term also applies to a stew of *langouste* or spiny lobster.

clarify   Method of removing impurities such as fat and scum from liquids, as well as foods such as butter. Stocks and soups, after being degreased, are generally clarified by cooking briefly with egg whites and shells and then straining through cheesecloth.

cocido   A Spanish stew made with chickpeas, vegetables and various meats.

cocotte	A French fireproof, oval or round, heavy cooking dish similar to a casserole.
correct	Process of modifying or increasing a flavor by the addition of more salt, pepper or other seasonings.
court bouillon	A flavored liquid in which fish or shellfish are simmered. Very often the liquid includes wine and vegetables. It can be used for poaching fish or in making sauces.
daube	Method of cooking meat or poultry slowly in a red wine stock with vegetables and seasonings. Also the name of a stew prepared in this manner.
deglaze	To dissolve the brown particles or pan drippings left in a pan by scraping and heating them with added liquid, generally water.
degrease	To remove the accumulated fat from the surface of stocks, soups or stews by either of two methods. From hot liquids, the fat is skimmed off with a spoon or skimmer; or the liquid can be cooled and put in the refrigerator, uncovered, until the fat hardens and can be scraped off.
dredge	To sprinkle food with flour, sugar or some other dry ingredients.
dutch oven	A large heavy kettle or pot with a tight-fitting lid, often made of cast iron. It is frequently used for making soups and stews.
estofado	A stew popular in Spain and South America.
estouffat	A stew popular in the Languedoc region of France. Its primary ingredients are generally dried beans and pork.
fines herbes	A mixture of chopped fresh and/or dried herbs, such as chives, parsley, tarragon and chervil, that is used to flavor soups, stews and other foods.

flambé	Method of setting a dish afire by pouring flaming brandy or another liquor over it and lighting it before the cooking process or just before serving. The alcohol burns off, leaving a desirable flavor.
fricassee	Method of preparing poultry by stewing slowly, then adding a white sauce. The term once meant any stew made with pieces of poultry, meat, fish or vegetables, and cooked in a brown or white stock.
goulash	A Hungarian stew made with varying ingredients, but generally flavored with paprika and very often with sour cream.
haricot	Small white bean, dried or fresh, often used in soups and stews from France.
hotch-potch	One of several similar names given to thick soups or stews made of various ingredients and which are enjoyed in several European countries. Among them are the English hot pot, Scotch hotch potch, Dutch *hutspot* and French *hochepot*.
lard	To insert strips of fat *(lardoons)* into lean meat before cooking to make it more juicy. This is done generally with a larding needle.
marinade	A seasoned liquid mixture in which food is soaked in order to tenderize it or to add further flavor.
marmite	A very large metal or earthenware French cooking pot that is used for making stocks and soups.
marrowbone	A large beef bone that holds a fatty filling called marrow. It is excellent for enriching such dishes as stocks, soups and stews.
matelote	A fish stew flavored with red or white wine.
miroton	A type of French stew made with cooked meat and flavored with onions.

navarin	A French lamb or mutton stew made with small onions and potatoes or with a variety of vegetables.
olla podrida	A hearty national Spanish soup or stew made with a great variety of ingredients, including several kinds of meat.
osso buco	An Italian stew whose name means literally "hollow bone." Its primary ingredients are veal shanks that are cooked in wine and stock with onions and tomatoes.
oxtail	An ox or beef tail, rich in flavor and highly prized for soups and stews.
pot-au-feu	A method of preparing soup or stew that yields a clear broth, meat and vegetables, each generally served separately.
purée	Food that has been cooked until very soft and then put through a sieve, ricer or blender. Also a thick soup made with puréed vegetables and a liquid.
ragoût	A stew of meat, poultry or fish, and sometimes with vegetables, that is generally highly seasoned.
ratatouille	A well-seasoned vegetable stew that is popular in Southern France and some other Mediterranean locales. It can be cooked on top of the stove or in the oven.
reduce	To cook a liquid over high heat until it is reduced in volume to give it the desired concentrated flavor.
render	To melt down a substance such as fat.
roux	A mixture of flour and fat cooked together and used to thicken such dishes as soups and stews. For a white *roux* the flour is not cooked until it turns brown as it is for a brown *roux*. A blond *roux* is pale gold and made only with butter.
sauté	To brown food in a small quantity of hot fat usually in an open pan or skillet.

sear	To brown the outside of food, especially meats, sealing in the juices and flavors. This is done by frying in hot fat or roasting in a hot oven.
simmer	To cook food gently in a liquid at just below the boiling point, at a temperature of about 185°F.
skim	To remove the accumulated fat and/or scum from the top of a liquid with a slotted spoon or skimmer.
stew	To cook in a liquid, covered, at low heat for a long period of time. A stew can be brown or white. For the former the meat is browned before the liquid is added. For a white stew the meat is put into cold liquid and then heated.
stifado	A Greek stew made with beef or lamb, small white onions, and cooked in a rich garlic and spice-flavored stock.
stock	The rich liquid that is obtained from the simmering together of meat, poultry, seafood, vegetables, and usually some bones, in seasoned water.
thickening agent	One or more foods, such as flour, cornstarch, arrowroot, egg yolk, *beurre*

INDEX

A CATALOGUE OF SELECTED DOVER BOOKS
IN ALL FIELDS OF INTEREST

A CATALOGUE OF SELECTED DOVER BOOKS
IN ALL FIELDS OF INTEREST

THE NOTEBOOKS OF LEONARDO DA VINCI, edited by J.P. Richter. Extracts from manuscripts reveal great genius; on painting, sculpture, anatomy, sciences, geography, etc. Both Italian and English. 186 ms. pages reproduced, plus 500 additional drawings, including studies for Last Supper, Sforza monument, etc. 860pp. 7⅞ x 10¾. USO 22572-0, 22573-9 Pa., Two vol. set $15.90

ART NOUVEAU DESIGNS IN COLOR, Alphonse Mucha, Maurice Verneuil, Georges Auriol. Full-color reproduction of Combinaisons ornamentales (c. 1900) by Art Nouveau masters. Floral, animal, geometric, interlacings, swashes — borders, frames, spots — all incredibly beautiful. 60 plates, hundreds of designs. 9⅜ x 8¹/₁₆. 22885-1 Pa. $4.00

GRAPHIC WORKS OF ODILON REDON. All great fantastic lithographs, etchings, engravings, drawings, 209 in all. Monsters, Huysmans, still life work, etc. Introduction by Alfred Werner. 209pp. 9⅛ x 12¼. 21996-8 Pa. $6.00

EXOTIC FLORAL PATTERNS IN COLOR, E.-A. Seguy. Incredibly beautiful full-color pochoir work by great French designer of 20's. Complete Bouquets et frondaisons, Suggestions pour étoffes. Richness must be seen to be believed. 40 plates containing 120 patterns. 80pp. 9⅜ x 12¼. 23041-4 Pa. $6.00

SELECTED ETCHINGS OF JAMES A. McN. WHISTLER, James A. McN. Whistler. 149 outstanding etchings by the great American artist, including selections from the Thames set and two Venice sets, the complete French set, and many individual prints. Introduction and explanatory note on each print by Maria Naylor. 157pp. 9⅜ x 12¼. 23194-1 Pa. $5.00

VISUAL ILLUSIONS: THEIR CAUSES, CHARACTERISTICS, AND APPLICATIONS, Matthew Luckiesh. Thorough description, discussion; shape and size, color, motion; natural illusion. Uses in art and industry. 100 illustrations. 252pp. 21530-X Pa. $3.00

TEN BOOKS ON ARCHITECTURE, Vitruvius. The most important book ever written on architecture. Early Roman aesthetics, technology, classical orders, site selection, all other aspects. Stands behind everything since. Morgan translation. 331pp. 20645-9 Pa. $3.75

THE CODEX NUTTALL. A PICTURE MANUSCRIPT FROM ANCIENT MEXICO, as first edited by Zelia Nuttall. Only inexpensive edition, in full color, of a pre-Columbian Mexican (Mixtec) book. 88 color plates show kings, gods, heroes, temples, sacrifices. New explanatory, historical introduction by Arthur G. Miller. 96pp. 11⅜ x 8½. 23168-2 Pa. $7.50

THE ART DECO STYLE, ed. by Theodore Menten. Furniture, jewelry, metalwork, ceramics, fabrics, lighting fixtures, interior decors, exteriors, graphics from pure French sources. Best sampling around. Over 400 photographs. 183pp. 8⅜ x 11¼.
22824-X Pa. $4.00

THE GENTLEMAN AND CABINET MAKER'S DIRECTOR, Thomas Chippendale. Full reprint, 1762 style book, most influential of all time; chairs, tables, sofas, mirrors, cabinets, etc. 200 plates, plus 24 photographs of surviving pieces. 249pp. 9⅞ x 12¾.
21601-2 Pa. $6.00

PINE FURNITURE OF EARLY NEW ENGLAND, Russell H. Kettell. Basic book. Thorough historical text, plus 200 illustrations of boxes, highboys, candlesticks, desks, etc. 477pp. 7⅞ x 10¾.
20145-7 Clothbd. $12.50

ORIENTAL RUGS, ANTIQUE AND MODERN, Walter A. Hawley. Persia, Turkey, Caucasus, Central Asia, China, other traditions. Best general survey of all aspects: styles and periods, manufacture, uses, symbols and their interpretation, and identification. 96 illustrations, 11 in color. 320pp. 6⅛ x 9¼.
22366-3 Pa. $5.00

DECORATIVE ANTIQUE IRONWORK, Henry R. d'Allemagne. Photographs of 4500 iron artifacts from world's finest collection, Rouen. Hinges, locks, candelabra, weapons, lighting devices, clocks, tools, from Roman times to mid-19th century. Nothing else comparable to it. 420pp. 9 x 12.
22082-6 Pa. $8.50

THE COMPLETE BOOK OF DOLL MAKING AND COLLECTING, Catherine Christopher. Instructions, patterns for dozens of dolls, from rag doll on up to elaborate, historically accurate figures. Mould faces, sew clothing, make doll houses, etc. Also collecting information. Many illustrations. 288pp. 6 x 9. 22066-4 Pa. $3.00

ANTIQUE PAPER DOLLS: 1915-1920, edited by Arnold Arnold. 7 antique cut-out dolls and 24 costumes from 1915-1920, selected by Arnold Arnold from his collection of rare children's books and entertainments, all in full color. 32pp. 9¼ x 12¼.
23176-3 Pa. $2.00

ANTIQUE PAPER DOLLS: THE EDWARDIAN ERA, Epinal. Full-color reproductions of two historic series of paper dolls that show clothing styles in 1908 and at the beginning of the First World War. 8 two-sided, stand-up dolls and 32 complete, two-sided costumes. Full instructions for assembling included. 32pp. 9¼ x 12¼.
23175-5 Pa. $2.00

A HISTORY OF COSTUME, Carl Köhler, Emma von Sichardt. Egypt, Babylon, Greece up through 19th century Europe; based on surviving pieces, art works, etc. Full text and 595 illustrations, including many clear, measured patterns for reproducing historic costume. Practical. 464pp. 21030-8 Pa. $4.00

EARLY AMERICAN LOCOMOTIVES, John H. White, Jr. Finest locomotive engravings from late 19th century: historical (1804-1874), main-line (after 1870), special, foreign, etc. 147 plates. 200pp. 11⅜ x 8¼. 22772-3 Pa. $3.50

SLEEPING BEAUTY, illustrated by Arthur Rackham. Perhaps the fullest, most delightful version ever, told by C.S. Evans. Rackham's best work. 49 illustrations. 110pp. 7⅞ x 10¾. 22756-1 Pa. $2.00

THE WONDERFUL WIZARD OF OZ, L. Frank Baum. Facsimile in full color of America's finest children's classic. Introduction by Martin Gardner. 143 illustrations by W.W. Denslow. 267pp. 20691-2 Pa. $3.50

GOOPS AND HOW TO BE THEM, Gelett Burgess. Classic tongue-in-cheek masquerading as etiquette book. 87 verses, 170 cartoons as Goops demonstrate virtues of table manners, neatness, courtesy, more. 88pp. 6½ x 9¼. 22233-0 Pa. $2.00

THE BROWNIES, THEIR BOOK, Palmer Cox. Small as mice, cunning as foxes, exuberant, mischievous, Brownies go to zoo, toy shop, seashore, circus, more. 24 verse adventures. 266 illustrations. 144pp. 6⅝ x 9¼. 21265-3 Pa. $2.50

BILLY WHISKERS: THE AUTOBIOGRAPHY OF A GOAT, Frances Trego Montgomery. Escapades of that rambunctious goat. Favorite from turn of the century America. 24 illustrations. 259pp. 22345-0 Pa. $2.75

THE ROCKET BOOK, Peter Newell. Fritz, janitor's kid, sets off rocket in basement of apartment house; an ingenious hole punched through every page traces course of rocket. 22 duotone drawings, verses. 48pp. 6⅞ x 8⅜. 22044-3 Pa. $1.50

CUT AND COLOR PAPER MASKS, Michael Grater. Clowns, animals, funny faces ... simply color them in, cut them out, and put them together, and you have 9 paper masks to play with and enjoy. Complete instructions. Assembled masks shown in full color on the covers. 32pp. 8¼ x 11. 23171-2 Pa. $1.50

THE TALE OF PETER RABBIT, Beatrix Potter. The inimitable Peter's terrifying adventure in Mr. McGregor's garden, with all 27 wonderful, full-color Potter illustrations. 55pp. 4¼ x 5½. USO 22827-4 Pa. $1.00

THE TALE OF MRS. TIGGY-WINKLE, Beatrix Potter. Your child will love this story about a very special hedgehog and all 27 wonderful, full-color Potter illustrations. 57pp. 4¼ x 5½. USO 20546-0 Pa. $1.00

THE TALE OF BENJAMIN BUNNY, Beatrix Potter. Peter Rabbit's cousin coaxes him back into Mr. McGregor's garden for a whole new set of adventures. A favorite with children. All 27 full-color illustrations. 59pp. 4¼ x 5½. USO 21102-9 Pa. $1.00

THE MERRY ADVENTURES OF ROBIN HOOD, Howard Pyle. Facsimile of original (1883) edition, finest modern version of English outlaw's adventures. 23 illustrations by Pyle. 296pp. 6½ x 9¼. 22043-5 Pa. $4.00

TWO LITTLE SAVAGES, Ernest Thompson Seton. Adventures of two boys who lived as Indians; explaining Indian ways, woodlore, pioneer methods. 293 illustrations. 286pp. 20985-7 Pa. $3.50

MANUAL OF THE TREES OF NORTH AMERICA, Charles S. Sargent. The basic survey of every native tree and tree-like shrub, 717 species in all. Extremely full descriptions, information on habitat, growth, locales, economics, etc. Necessary to every serious tree lover. Over 100 finding keys. 783 illustrations. Total of 986pp.
20277-1, 20278-X Pa., Two vol. set $9.00

BIRDS OF THE NEW YORK AREA, John Bull. Indispensable guide to more than 400 species within a hundred-mile radius of Manhattan. Information on range, status, breeding, migration, distribution trends, etc. Foreword by Roger Tory Peterson. 17 drawings; maps. 540pp.
23222-0 Pa. $6.00

THE SEA-BEACH AT EBB-TIDE, Augusta Foote Arnold. Identify hundreds of marine plants and animals: algae, seaweeds, squids, crabs, corals, etc. Descriptions cover food, life cycle, size, shape, habitat. Over 600 drawings. 490pp.
21949-6 Pa. $5.00

THE MOTH BOOK, William J. Holland. Identify more than 2,000 moths of North America. General information, precise species descriptions. 623 illustrations plus 48 color plates show almost all species, full size. 1968 edition. Still the basic book. Total of 551pp. 6½ x 9¼.
21948-8 Pa. $6.00

HOW INDIANS USE WILD PLANTS FOR FOOD, MEDICINE & CRAFTS, Frances Densmore. Smithsonian, Bureau of American Ethnology report presents wealth of material on nearly 200 plants used by Chippewas of Minnesota and Wisconsin. 33 plates plus 122pp. of text. 6⅛ x 9¼.
23019-8 Pa. $2.50

OLD NEW YORK IN EARLY PHOTOGRAPHS, edited by Mary Black. Your only chance to see New York City as it was 1853-1906, through 196 wonderful photographs from N.Y. Historical Society. Great Blizzard, Lincoln's funeral procession, great buildings. 228pp. 9 x 12.
22907-6 Pa. $6.95

THE AMERICAN REVOLUTION, A PICTURE SOURCEBOOK, John Grafton. Wonderful Bicentennial picture source, with 411 illustrations (contemporary and 19th century) showing battles, personalities, maps, events, flags, posters, soldier's life, ships, etc. all captioned and explained. A wonderful browsing book, supplement to other historical reading. 160pp. 9 x 12.
23226-3 Pa. $4.00

PERSONAL NARRATIVE OF A PILGRIMAGE TO AL-MADINAH AND MECCAH, Richard Burton. Great travel classic by remarkably colorful personality. Burton, disguised as a Moroccan, visited sacred shrines of Islam, narrowly escaping death. Wonderful observations of Islamic life, customs, personalities. 47 illustrations. Total of 959pp.
21217-3, 21218-1 Pa., Two vol. set $10.00

INCIDENTS OF TRAVEL IN CENTRAL AMERICA, CHIAPAS, AND YUCATAN, John L. Stephens. Almost single-handed discovery of Maya culture; exploration of ruined cities, monuments, temples; customs of Indians. 115 drawings. 892pp.
22404-X, 22405-8 Pa., Two vol. set $9.00

CREATIVE LITHOGRAPHY AND HOW TO DO IT, Grant Arnold. Lithography as art form: working directly on stone, transfer of drawings, lithotint, mezzotint, color printing; also metal plates. Detailed, thorough. 27 illustrations. 214pp.
21208-4 Pa. $3.50

DESIGN MOTIFS OF ANCIENT MEXICO, Jorge Enciso. Vigorous, powerful ceramic stamp impressions — Maya, Aztec, Toltec, Olmec. Serpents, gods, priests, dancers, etc. 153pp. 6⅛ x 9¼.
20084-1 Pa. $2.50

AMERICAN INDIAN DESIGN AND DECORATION, Leroy Appleton. Full text, plus more than 700 precise drawings of Inca, Maya, Aztec, Pueblo, Plains, NW Coast basketry, sculpture, painting, pottery, sand paintings, metal, etc. 4 plates in color. 279pp. 8⅜ x 11¼.
22704-9 Pa. $5.00

CHINESE LATTICE DESIGNS, Daniel S. Dye. Incredibly beautiful geometric designs: circles, voluted, simple dissections, etc. Inexhaustible source of ideas, motifs. 1239 illustrations. 469pp. 6⅛ x 9¼.
23096-1 Pa. $5.00

JAPANESE DESIGN MOTIFS, Matsuya Co. Mon, or heraldic designs. Over 4000 typical, beautiful designs: birds, animals, flowers, swords, fans, geometric; all beautifully stylized. 213pp. 11⅜ x 8¼.
22874-6 Pa. '$5.00

PERSPECTIVE, Jan Vredeman de Vries. 73 perspective plates from 1604 edition; buildings, townscapes, stairways, fantastic scenes. Remarkable for beauty, surrealistic atmosphere; real eye-catchers. Introduction by Adolf Placzek. 74pp. 11⅜ x 8¼.
20186-4 Pa. $3.00

EARLY AMERICAN DESIGN MOTIFS. Suzanne E. Chapman. 497 motifs, designs, from painting on wood, ceramics, appliqué, glassware, samplers, metal work, etc. Florals, landscapes, birds and animals, geometrics, letters, etc. Inexhaustible. Enlarged edition. 138pp. 8⅜ x 11¼.
22985-8 Pa. $3.50
23084-8 Clothbd. $7.95

VICTORIAN STENCILS FOR DESIGN AND DECORATION, edited by E.V. Gillon, Jr. 113 wonderful ornate Victorian pieces from German sources; florals, geometrics; borders, corner pieces; bird motifs, etc. 64pp. 9⅜ x 12¼.
21995-X Pa. $3.00

ART NOUVEAU: AN ANTHOLOGY OF DESIGN AND ILLUSTRATION FROM THE STUDIO, edited by E.V. Gillon, Jr. Graphic arts: book jackets, posters, engravings, illustrations, decorations; Crane, Beardsley, Bradley and many others. Inexhaustible. 92pp. 8⅛ x 11.
22388-4 Pa. $2.50

ORIGINAL ART DECO DESIGNS, William Rowe. First-rate, highly imaginative modern Art Deco frames, borders, compositions, alphabets, florals, insectals, Wurlitzer-types, etc. Much finest modern Art Deco. 80 plates, 8 in color. 8⅜ x 11¼.
22567-4 Pa. $3.50

HANDBOOK OF DESIGNS AND DEVICES, Clarence P. Hornung. Over 1800 basic geometric designs based on circle, triangle, square, scroll, cross, etc. Largest such collection in existence. 261pp.
20125-2 Pa. $2.75

THE FITZWILLIAM VIRGINAL BOOK, edited by J. Fuller Maitland, W.B. Squire. Famous early 17th century collection of keyboard music, 300 works by Morley, Byrd, Bull, Gibbons, etc. Modern notation. Total of 938pp. 8⅜ x 11.
ECE 21068-5, 21069-3 Pa., Two vol. set $15.00

COMPLETE STRING QUARTETS, Wolfgang A. Mozart. Breitkopf and Härtel edition. All 23 string quartets plus alternate slow movement to K156. Study score. 277pp. 9⅜ x 12¼.
22372-8 Pa. $6.00

COMPLETE SONG CYCLES, Franz Schubert. Complete piano, vocal music of Die Schöne Müllerin, Die Winterreise, Schwanengesang. Also Drinker English singing translations. Breitkopf and Härtel edition. 217pp. 9⅜ x 12¼.
22649-2 Pa. $5.00

THE COMPLETE PRELUDES AND ETUDES FOR PIANOFORTE SOLO, Alexander Scriabin. All the preludes and etudes including many perfectly spun miniatures. Edited by K.N. Igumnov and Y.I. Mil'shteyn. 250pp. 9 x 12.
22919-X Pa. $6.00

TRISTAN UND ISOLDE, Richard Wagner. Full orchestral score with complete instrumentation. Do not confuse with piano reduction. Commentary by Felix Mottl, great Wagnerian conductor and scholar. Study score. 655pp. 8⅛ x 11.
22915-7 Pa. $11.95

FAVORITE SONGS OF THE NINETIES, ed. Robert Fremont. Full reproduction, including covers, of 88 favorites: Ta-Ra-Ra-Boom-De-Aye, The Band Played On, Bird in a Gilded Cage, Under the Bamboo Tree, After the Ball, etc. 401pp. 9 x 12.
EBE 21536-9 Pa. $6.95

SOUSA'S GREAT MARCHES IN PIANO TRANSCRIPTION: ORIGINAL SHEET MUSIC OF 23 WORKS, John Philip Sousa. Selected by Lester S. Levy. Playing edition includes: The Stars and Stripes Forever, The Thunderer, The Gladiator, King Cotton, Washington Post, much more. 24 illustrations. 111pp. 9 x 12.
USO 23132-1 Pa. $3.50

CLASSIC PIANO RAGS, selected with an introduction by Rudi Blesh. Best ragtime music (1897-1922) by Scott Joplin, James Scott, Joseph F. Lamb, Tom Turpin, 9 others. Printed from best original sheet music, plus covers. 364pp. 9 x 12.
EBE 20469-3 Pa. $7.50

ANALYSIS OF CHINESE CHARACTERS, C.D. Wilder, J.H. Ingram. 1000 most important characters analyzed according to primitives, phonetics, historical development. Traditional method offers mnemonic aid to beginner, intermediate student of Chinese, Japanese. 365pp.
23045-7 Pa. $4.00

MODERN CHINESE: A BASIC COURSE, Faculty of Peking University. Self study, classroom course in modern Mandarin. Records contain phonetics, vocabulary, sentences, lessons. 249 page book contains all recorded text, translations, grammar, vocabulary, exercises. Best course on market. 3 12" 33⅓ monaural records, book, album.
98832-5 Set $12.50

AUSTRIAN COOKING AND BAKING, Gretel Beer. Authentic thick soups, wiener schnitzel, veal goulash, more, plus dumplings, puff pastries, nut cakes, sacher tortes, other great Austrian desserts. 224pp. USO 23220-4 Pa. $2.50

CHEESES OF THE WORLD, U.S.D.A. Dictionary of cheeses containing descriptions of over 400 varieties of cheese from common Cheddar to exotic Surati. Up to two pages are given to important cheeses like Camembert, Cottage, Edam, etc. 151pp. 22831-2 Pa. $1.50

TRITTON'S GUIDE TO BETTER WINE AND BEER MAKING FOR BEGINNERS, S.M. Tritton. All you need to know to make family-sized quantities of over 100 types of grape, fruit, herb, vegetable wines; plus beers, mead, cider, more. 11 illustrations. 157pp. USO 22528-3 Pa. $2.25

DECORATIVE LABELS FOR HOME CANNING, PRESERVING, AND OTHER HOUSEHOLD AND GIFT USES, Theodore Menten. 128 gummed, perforated labels, beautifully printed in 2 colors. 12 versions in traditional, Art Nouveau, Art Deco styles. Adhere to metal, glass, wood, most plastics. 24pp. 8¼ x 11. 23219-0 Pa. $2.00

FIVE ACRES AND INDEPENDENCE, Maurice G. Kains. Great back-to-the-land classic explains basics of self-sufficient farming: economics, plants, crops, animals, orchards, soils, land selection, host of other necessary things. Do not confuse with skimpy faddist literature; Kains was one of America's greatest agriculturalists. 95 illustrations. 397pp. 20974-1 Pa. $3.00

GROWING VEGETABLES IN THE HOME GARDEN, U.S. Dept. of Agriculture. Basic information on site, soil conditions, selection of vegetables, planting, cultivation, gathering. Up-to-date, concise, authoritative. Covers 60 vegetables. 30 illustrations. 123pp. 23167-4 Pa. $1.35

FRUITS FOR THE HOME GARDEN, Dr. U.P. Hedrick. A chapter covering each type of garden fruit, advice on plant care, soils, grafting, pruning, sprays, transplanting, and much more! Very full. 53 illustrations. 175pp. 22944-0 Pa. $2.50

GARDENING ON SANDY SOIL IN NORTH TEMPERATE AREAS, Christine Kelway. Is your soil too light, too sandy? Improve your soil, select plants that survive under such conditions. Both vegetables and flowers. 42 photos. 148pp. USO 23199-2 Pa. $2.50

THE FRAGRANT GARDEN: A BOOK ABOUT SWEET SCENTED FLOWERS AND LEAVES, Louise Beebe Wilder. Fullest, best book on growing plants for their fragrances. Descriptions of hundreds of plants, both well-known and overlooked. 407pp. 23071-6 Pa. **$4.00**

EASY GARDENING WITH DROUGHT-RESISTANT PLANTS, Arno and Irene Nehrling. Authoritative guide to gardening with plants that require a minimum of water: seashore, desert, and rock gardens; house plants; annuals and perennials; much more. 190 illustrations. 320pp. 23230-1 Pa. $3.50

MODERN CHESS STRATEGY, Ludek Pachman. The use of the queen, the active king, exchanges, pawn play, the center, weak squares, etc. Section on rook alone worth price of the book. Stress on the moderns. Often considered the most important book on strategy. 314pp. 20290-9 Pa. $3.50

CHESS STRATEGY, Edward Lasker. One of half-dozen great theoretical works in chess, shows principles of action above and beyond moves. Acclaimed by Capablanca, Keres, etc. 282pp. USO 20528-2 Pa. $3.00

CHESS PRAXIS, THE PRAXIS OF MY SYSTEM, Aron Nimzovich. Founder of hypermodern chess explains his profound, influential theories that have dominated much of 20th century chess. 109 illustrative games. 369pp. 20296-8 Pa. $3.50

HOW TO PLAY THE CHESS OPENINGS, Eugene Znosko-Borovsky. Clear, profound examinations of just what each opening is intended to do and how opponent can counter. Many sample games, questions and answers. 147pp. 22795-2 Pa. $2.00

THE ART OF CHESS COMBINATION, Eugene Znosko-Borovsky. Modern explanation of principles, varieties, techniques and ideas behind them, illustrated with many examples from great players. 212pp. 20583-5 Pa. $2.50

COMBINATIONS: THE HEART OF CHESS, Irving Chernev. Step-by-step explanation of intricacies of combinative play. 356 combinations by Tarrasch, Botvinnik, Keres, Steinitz, Anderssen, Morphy, Marshall, Capablanca, others, all annotated. 245 pp. 21744-2 Pa. $3.00

HOW TO PLAY CHESS ENDINGS, Eugene Znosko-Borovsky. Thorough instruction manual by fine teacher analyzes each piece individually; many common endgame situations. Examines games by Steinitz, Alekhine, Lasker, others. Emphasis on understanding. 288pp. 21170-3 Pa. $2.75

MORPHY'S GAMES OF CHESS, Philip W. Sergeant. Romantic history, 54 games of greatest player of all time against Anderssen, Bird, Paulsen, Harrwitz; 52 games at odds; 52 blindfold; 100 consultation, informal, other games. Analyses by Anderssen, Steinitz, Morphy himself. 352pp. 20386-7 Pa. $4.00

500 MASTER GAMES OF CHESS, S. Tartakower, J. du Mont. Vast collection of great chess games from 1798-1938, with much material nowhere else readily available. Fully annotated, arranged by opening for easier study. 665pp. 23208-5 Pa. $6.00

THE SOVIET SCHOOL OF CHESS, Alexander Kotov and M. Yudovich. Authoritative work on modern Russian chess. History, conceptual background. 128 fully annotated games (most unavailable elsewhere) by Botvinnik, Keres, Smyslov, Tal, Petrosian, Spassky, more. 390pp. 20026-4 Pa. $3.95

WONDERS AND CURIOSITIES OF CHESS, Irving Chernev. A lifetime's accumulation of such wonders and curiosities as the longest won game, shortest game, chess problem with mate in 1220 moves, and much more unusual material —356 items in all, over 160 complete games. 146 diagrams. 203pp. 23007-4 Pa. $3.50

EARLY NEW ENGLAND GRAVESTONE RUBBINGS, Edmund V. Gillon, Jr. 43 photographs, 226 rubbings show heavily symbolic, macabre, sometimes humorous primitive American art. Up to early 19th century. 207pp. 8⅜ x 11¼.
21380-3 Pa. $4.00

L.J.M. DAGUERRE: THE HISTORY OF THE DIORAMA AND THE DAGUERREOTYPE, Helmut and Alison Gernsheim. Definitive account. Early history, life and work of Daguerre; discovery of daguerreotype process; diffusion abroad; other early photography. 124 illustrations. 226pp. 6⅙ x 9¼.
22290-X Pa. $4.00

PHOTOGRAPHY AND THE AMERICAN SCENE, Robert Taft. The basic book on American photography as art, recording form, 1839-1889. Development, influence on society, great photographers, types (portraits, war, frontier, etc.), whatever else needed. Inexhaustible. Illustrated with 322 early photos, daguerreotypes, tintypes, stereo slides, etc. 546pp. 6⅛ x 9¼.
21201-7 Pa. $6.00

PHOTOGRAPHIC SKETCHBOOK OF THE CIVIL WAR, Alexander Gardner. Reproduction of 1866 volume with 100 on-the-field photographs: Manassas, Lincoln on battlefield, slave pens, etc. Introduction by E.F. Bleiler. 224pp. 10¾ x 9.
22731-6 Pa. $6.00

THE MOVIES: A PICTURE QUIZ BOOK, Stanley Appelbaum & Hayward Cirker. Match stars with their movies, name actors and actresses, test your movie skill with 241 stills from 236 great movies, 1902-1959. Indexes of performers and films. 128pp. 8⅜ x 9¼.
20222-4 Pa. $3.00

THE TALKIES, Richard Griffith. Anthology of features, articles from Photoplay, 1928-1940, reproduced complete. Stars, famous movies, technical features, fabulous ads, etc.; Garbo, Chaplin, King Kong, Lubitsch, etc. 4 color plates, scores of illustrations. 327pp. 8⅜ x 11¼.
22762-6 Pa. $6.95

THE MOVIE MUSICAL FROM VITAPHONE TO "42ND STREET," edited by Miles Kreuger. Relive the rise of the movie musical as reported in the pages of Photoplay magazine (1926-1933): every movie review, cast list, ad, and record review; every significant feature article, production still, biography, forecast, and gossip story. Profusely illustrated. 367pp. 8⅜ x 11¼.
23154-2 Pa. $7.95

JOHANN SEBASTIAN BACH, Philipp Spitta. Great classic of biography, musical commentary, with hundreds of pieces analyzed. Also good for Bach's contemporaries. 450 musical examples. Total of 1799pp.
EUK 22278-0, 22279-9 Clothbd., Two vol. set $25.00

BEETHOVEN AND HIS NINE SYMPHONIES, Sir George Grove. Thorough history, analysis, commentary on symphonies and some related pieces. For either beginner or advanced student. 436 musical passages. 407pp.
20334-4 Pa. $4.00

MOZART AND HIS PIANO CONCERTOS, Cuthbert Girdlestone. The only full-length study. Detailed analyses of all 21 concertos, sources; 417 musical examples. 509pp.
21271-8 Pa. $6.00

EGYPTIAN MAGIC, E.A. Wallis Budge. Foremost Egyptologist, curator at British Museum, on charms, curses, amulets, doll magic, transformations, control of demons, deific appearances, feats of great magicians. Many texts cited. 19 illustrations. 234pp.   USO 22681-6 Pa. $2.50

THE LEYDEN PAPYRUS: AN EGYPTIAN MAGICAL BOOK, edited by F. Ll. Griffith, Herbert Thompson. Egyptian sorcerer's manual contains scores of spells: sex magic of various sorts, occult information, evoking visions, removing evil magic, etc. Transliteration faces translation. 207pp.   22994-7 Pa. $2.50

THE MALLEUS MALEFICARUM OF KRAMER AND SPRENGER, translated, edited by Montague Summers. Full text of most important witchhunter's "Bible," used by both Catholics and Protestants. Theory of witches, manifestations, remedies, etc. Indispensable to serious student. 278pp. 6⅝ x 10.   USO 22802-9 Pa. $3.95

LOST CONTINENTS, L. Sprague de Camp. Great science-fiction author, finest, fullest study: Atlantis, Lemuria, Mu, Hyperborea, etc. Lost Tribes, Irish in pre-Columbian America, root races; in history, literature, art, occultism. Necessary to everyone concerned with theme. 17 illustrations. 348pp.   22668-9 Pa. $3.50

THE COMPLETE BOOKS OF CHARLES FORT, Charles Fort. Book of the Damned, Lo!, Wild Talents, New Lands. Greatest compilation of data: celestial appearances, flying saucers, falls of frogs, strange disappearances, inexplicable data not recognized by science. Inexhaustible, painstakingly documented. Do not confuse with modern charlatanry. Introduction by Damon Knight. Total of 1126pp.
23094-5 Clothbd. $15.00

FADS AND FALLACIES IN THE NAME OF SCIENCE, Martin Gardner. Fair, witty appraisal of cranks and quacks of science: Atlantis, Lemuria, flat earth, Velikovsky, orgone energy, Bridey Murphy, medical fads, etc. 373pp.   20394-8 Pa. $3.50

HOAXES, Curtis D. MacDougall. Unbelievably rich account of great hoaxes: Locke's moon hoax, Shakespearean forgeries, Loch Ness monster, Disumbrationist school of art, dozens more; also psychology of hoaxing. 54 illustrations. 338pp.   20465-0 Pa. $3.50

THE GENTLE ART OF MAKING ENEMIES, James A.M. Whistler. Greatest wit of his day deflates Wilde, Ruskin, Swinburne; strikes back at inane critics, exhibitions. Highly readable classic of impressionist revolution by great painter. Introduction by Alfred Werner. 334pp.   21875-9 Pa. $4.00

THE BOOK OF TEA, Kakuzo Okakura. Minor classic of the Orient: entertaining, charming explanation, interpretation of traditional Japanese culture in terms of tea ceremony. Edited by E.F. Bleiler. Total of 94pp.   20070-1 Pa. $1.25

Prices subject to change without notice.
Available at your book dealer or write for free catalogue to Dept. GI, Dover Publications, Inc., 180 Varick St., N.Y., N.Y. 10014. Dover publishes more than 150 books each year on science, elementary and advanced mathematics, biology, music, art, literary history, social sciences and other areas.